RIVER ROUGH,
RIVER SMOOTH

RIVER ROUGH, RIVER SMOOTH

Adventures on Manitoba's Historic Hayes River

Anthony Dalton

NATURAL HERITAGE BOOKS
A MEMBER OF THE DUNDURN GROUP
TORONTO

Published by Natural Heritage Books
A Member of The Dundurn Group

Edited by Shannon Whibbs
Design by Jennifer Scott
Printed and bound in Canada by Transcontinental.

Library and Archives Canada Cataloguing in Publication

Dalton, Anthony, 1940-
    River rough, river smooth : adventures on Manitoba's historic Hayes River / by Anthony Dalton.

Includes bibliographical references and index.
ISBN 978-1-55488-712-5

1. Dalton, Anthony, 1940- --Travel--Manitoba--Hayes River. 2. Hayes River (Man.)--Description and travel.
3. Hayes River (Man.)--History. I. Title.

FC3395.H38D35 2009   917.127'104   C2009-906936-9

1   2   3   4   5   14   13   12   11   10

Conseil des Arts du Canada / Canada Council for the Arts

Canadä

ONTARIO ARTS COUNCIL
CONSEIL DES ARTS DE L'ONTARIO

We acknowledge the support of the **Canada Council for the Arts** and the **Ontario Arts Council** for our publishing program. We also acknowledge the financial support of the **Government of Canada** through the **Book Publishing Industry Development Program** and **The Association for the Export of Canadian Books**, and the **Government of Ontario** through the **Ontario Book Publishers Tax Credit program**, and the **Ontario Media Development Corporation**.

Care has been taken to trace the ownership of copyright material used in this book. The author and the publisher welcome any information enabling them to rectify any references or credits in subsequent editions.

J. Kirk Howard, President

www.dundurn.com

Colour photos © Anthony Dalton Collection
Front cover photographs courtesy of the author.

Dundurn Press
3 Church Street, Suite 500
Toronto, Ontario, Canada
M5E 1M2

Gazelle Book Services Limited
White Cross Mills
High Town, Lancaster, England
LA1 4XS

Dundurn Press
2250 Military Road
Tonawanda, NY
U.S.A. 14150

For Steve Crowhurst and Graeme Halley

"All my life," he said, "I have searched for the treasure. I have sought it in the high places, and in the narrow. I have sought it in deep jungles, and at the ends of rivers, and in dark caverns — and yet have not found it.

"Instead, at the end of every trail, I have found you awaiting me. And now you have become familiar to me, though I cannot say I know you well.
Who are you?"

And the stranger answered:
"Thyself."

— *From an old tale*[1]

CONTENTS

PREFACE

Since I was a boy, roaming alone across a deserted Second-World-War aerodrome[1] in southern England on foot or on my bicycle in search of wild creatures, or building a makeshift raft out of oil drums and old rope and paddling across a flooded gravel quarry, I have felt at home in the outdoors. In those long-gone years, when not at school, my days varied between solitary adventures and reading about the travels of larger-than-life figures from history and from fiction. Books by H. Rider Haggard, G.A. Henty, and R. M. Ballantyne adorned my bookshelves. Later, as I grew older and my literary education improved, I found much satisfaction in the heroic deeds as told by the masters of Greek mythology. Homer in particular thrilled me with his dramatic opus *The Iliad* and his glorious tale of the epic journey undertaken by Ulysses in *The Odyssey*. Equally, I was inspired by the magnificent prose poems crafted by Samuel Taylor Coleridge, John Keats, Henry Wordsworth Longfellow, Sir Walter Scott, and Alfred Lord Tennyson, plus the controversial but brilliant Charles Beaudelaire.

Those feelings of youthful comfort in the outdoors, combined with the books I devoured, eventually translated into a nomadic adult life of adventure that has taken me across great deserts, into the high mountains, through steamy jungles, down mighty rivers, and over the world's seas. By the early 1990s I had travelled just about everywhere I wanted to go, and I had a memory bank full of extremely personal treasures. For these reasons I included the three enigmatic paragraphs from an old tale by an unknown author[2] to open this book. Those few words, more than perhaps any others, could reflect the possible raison d'être for my many long journeys, including the two related in this collection.

From my earliest years the sea held a fascination for me that I could never deny. Perhaps that had much to do with being born in Gravesend, on the south bank of the Thames estuary — in its lower reaches, one of the most important commercial rivers in the world. Every day a never-ending parade of ships of all sizes and from all maritime nations steamed up and down the river, to and from Tilbury Docks and the Pool of London. As a small boy, whenever I could, I watched from the shore and dreamed of faraway places.

In direct contrast to the sea, following an extended visit to Egypt, Sudan, and Libya, followed by the equally sand-covered lands of Syria, Jordan, and Iraq in my early twenties, I developed a passion for deserts. As a direct result of that initial North African and Middle Eastern experience, I later spent much time exploring the western and central Sahara, the incredibly beautiful Namib, much more of the Middle East, and the barren parts of the Australian Outback. Most years, my love of boats and being on the water fitted comfortably in between desert journeys.

Despite my devotion to the deserts and seas of the world, often when back home in Canada I would study maps of the North. In the late 1970s and mid 1980s I travelled in the Arctic a few times and knew I wanted to see more. Equally, I was fascinated by the barren lands between the populated southern corridor across

Canada and the Arctic Circle. The great rivers, in particular, called out to me, perhaps inspired by my early years on the banks of the Thames. Tales of the adventures lived by the hardy fur traders and explorers of the Hudson's Bay Company intrigued me. I knew that one day, when I had had my fill of deserts, I would roam north and see more of Canada.

In 1992 I visited Churchill, Manitoba, on a photojournalism assignment. There, on the shores of Hudson Bay, I met Mark Ingebrigtson. Mark, owner of a local travel agency, loaned me his truck so I could go exploring on my own. He arranged for me to take a helicopter flight over the Hudson Bay shoreline in search of polar bears. He and a fellow photographer, Mike Macri, showed me Churchill and its environs in a way that few could. Across the Churchill River, easily visible from where I watched beluga whales cruising in from the bay, stood the concrete bulk of Fort Prince of Wales: once a bastion of the Hudson's Bay Company.

Eighteen months later Mark's friend and business associate, Rob Bruce-Barron, a marketing advisor to a variety of Manitoba organizations, contacted me with an offer I could not resist. A team of Cree First Nation rowers from Norway House were planning to take a replica of a traditional York boat down the full length of the Hayes River to York Factory in the summer of 1994. Would I like to go with them to document the expedition? Would I? You bet I would.

At that time I was living in Antwerp,[3] Belgium. Manitoba and Norway House were on the other side of an ocean. Fortunately, I had a few months in which to make arrangements. Between other writing and photography jobs, I studied maps of Manitoba, I read about the Hudson's Bay Company's use of the Hayes River, and I learned how York boats were built. I still had no idea what I was getting myself into. I just knew I had to be a part of that historic voyage.

River Rough, River Smooth is, for the most part, the remarkable story of an expedition on an historic Canadian river that started full

York Factory as it looked in 1853. The author's goal was to reach York Factory by travelling the full length of the Hayes River.

of promise, yet failed because, I suspect, the reality of the journey was considerably more demanding than the dream that inspired it. The original expedition by York boat was terminated less than half the way down the Hayes River. That rather abrupt ending of what could have continued as a great adventure for all of us on board saddened me deeply. However, I had committed myself to travelling 650 kilometres on the Hayes River and, despite the unexpected change of plans at Oxford House in 1994 and again in 1995, I was determined to continue the journey one way or another. After a few false starts, six summers later I did just that. That journey, too, is part of this story, as are brief glimpses into life as it was for the river runners and other travellers during the fur-trade era.

I am grateful for the opportunity of challenging the Hayes River with the easygoing members of the Norway House York boat crew. Most of the time I enjoyed myself immensely and I learned so much from them. Equally, I can smile with satisfaction when I think of the later expedition by canoe: of my travelling companions and the adventures we shared on the next stage of that great river coursing across Manitoba to spill itself into

Hudson Bay. Both journeys were physically challenging. Both were important history lessons for me. In combination, they were another realization of some of my boyhood dreams.

ACKNOWLEDGEMENTS

Without the approval of Ken McKay, from Norway House, I would never have been offered the opportunity of taking part in the York boat expedition. We didn't always agree once we were on the river, but he has my respect and my extreme gratitude. I should also mention that I have the utmost admiration for his boat-building skills. In addition, I must offer my sincere thanks to the other members of the crew for allowing me to share their adventure. They are: Charlie Muchikekwanape, Wayne Simpson, Ryan Simpson, Gordon McKay, Edward Monias, Nathanial "Simon" Clynes, David Chubb Jr., Murray Balfour, John Wesley, Ken Ormand Sr., and Benjamin Paul. To a man, they demonstrated tenacity and absolute dedication to the task at hand. Their forefathers, the early Cree tripmen, would have been so proud of them. I would like to comment on the friendship that Charlie and Wayne showed me from the start in Norway House and during our time on the river. It was important to me and much appreciated. I know I am indebted to many other people of the

Cree First Nation from Norway House; most notably I would like to single out Irv Swanson and Albert Tait. Irv met me at the airstrip and introduced me to Norway House and the York boat crew. Albert befriended me, kept me amused with his nonstop jokes, and drove me around Norway House and the surrounding area. I enjoyed his company and will always regret that he was not able to join us on the river.

I am deeply grateful to Mark Ingebrigtson from Churchill for his support during a series of visits to Manitoba. Likewise, in Winnipeg, I owe thanks to Rob Bruce-Barron of CanZeal Ltd. who arranged for my journey with the Norway House York Boat Expedition, and, on two occasions, found room and a bed for me in his home. Over a few years, Denis Maksymetz at Travel Manitoba and Charles Hatzipanayis from Industry Canada gave me much leeway in my travels around their beautiful province and opened many important doors for me. I thank you both for your generosity. My thanks also to Tim Muskego and Neil Bradburn at Oxford House for their kindness to me while I waited in vain for the Norway House crew to arrive in 1995.

On the canoe run from Oxford House to York Factory, I thoroughly enjoyed the company of fellow author Barbara J. Scot, biologists Valerie Hodge and Herbert Koepp and, from Winnipeg-based Wilderness Spirit Adventures, the highly skilled and irrepressible duo of Rob Currie and Mark Loewen. Rob and Mark shared with us their enthusiasm for great Canadian rivers and their seemingly inexhaustible supply of humour. Thanks also to their partner and mentor, Bruno Rosenberg; and to the Discovery Channel television crew who joined us briefly late in the journey. The cooks at Knee Lake Lodge deserve credit and our gratitude for feeding six cold, wet, and weary voyagers one stormy evening. Eric Saunders of Silver Goose Camp Ltd. sent me useful information on York Factory, which I received with thanks. Finally, thanks to Air Canada for getting me to Winnipeg and home again.

Acknowledgements

As with a previous book dealing with Hudson's Bay Company history, I am extremely appreciative of the ever helpful staff at the Archives of Manitoba/HBC Archives in Winnipeg.

Some of my fellow writers in the Canadian Authors Association have given me so much encouragement over the past few years; they deserve mention, especially: Matthew Bin, Karen (kc) Dyer, Suzanne Harris, Margaret Hume, Jean Kay, Bernice Lever, Anita Purcell, Arlene Smith, and my favourite Irish author — Patrick Taylor. Thanks so much. You are special people.

My thanks to Barry Penhale of Natural Heritage Books (part of the Dundurn Group) for taking on this project and for his encouragement. Thanks also to Dundurn Group publisher Kirk Howard for accepting me into his publishing family. My editor, Shannon Whibbs, deserves special mention for her patience with me during the editing process and for her considerable editing skills. Thank you so much. I have enjoyed working with you, Shannon.

CHAPTER I
Rowing Down the River

There is no place to get to know companions more intimately than in a small craft on a voyage.
— Tristan Jones (1929–1995), *To Venture Further*

"AHA, BOYS! OHO, BOYS! Come on, boys! Let's go, boys!" Ken McKay's rich voice echoed down the wilderness river. A few crows took alarm. They cawed their disapproval and launched themselves skywards, flapping shiny, black wings urgently away from the intrusive cries. As Ken's words reverberated off the smooth, granite boulders on either side, eight strong backs bent over long, slim oars. Before his command had been completed, sixteen tired arms picked up the tempo. An equal number of legs braced against any solid object as dozens of muscles took up the strain. Eight oars sliced into the river as one.

Directly in front of me, Wayne Simpson's red oar blade bit deeply into the cold water, ripped through it, and burst up into the warmer air. Sparkling drops of the Hayes River spilled in a cascade of miniature jewels behind it. Without hesitation, the oar plunged to the river again to complete the cycle: and then to start all over again. For once oblivious to my surroundings, I followed, forcing my oar to mimic the one in front.

Wayne had been rowing regularly for much of the summer on Playgreen Lake, beside Norway House. I had enjoyed little recent practice. He was twenty-seven. I was fifty-four. The age difference was uncomfortably obvious, especially to me. My arms felt like lead as I fought to maintain his rhythm. Drop the blade into the river, force back hard, and lift out again. Into the river, force back hard, and lift out again. Over and over the brief monotonous cycle was repeated. My eyes focused on a point in the middle of Wayne's powerful shoulders, just below the collar of his white T-shirt, where the manufacturer's oblong label showed vaguely through the material. As he moved back, pulling hard on the oar, so I pulled back at the same time, desperately trying to keep time by maintaining a constant distance between my eyes and that arbitrary spot on his shirt.

I rarely took a seat at the oars. My job was photography and writing the expedition log. Cameras and oars are not compatible when used by one man at the same time. For the moment my cameras were safely stowed near my feet. Shutter speeds and apertures were far from my mind. Determined to row as hard and for as long as those around me; forcing myself not to be the first to rest his oar, I allowed my mind to slide into a different realm. Think rhythm. Think Baudelaire.

Bau-del-aire. Three short syllables. One for the blade's drop into the river. Another for the pressure against living water. The third — just as it sounds, I told myself — back into the air. Bau-del-aire. Bau-del-aire. Bau-del-aire.

Allons! Allons! Allons![1] *(Let's go on! Let's go on! Let's go on!)*

My rowing rhythm improved a little with the beat in my head. Subconsciously, silently, I recited the sensual lines from my favourite parts of Baudelaire's "Le Voyage":

Chaque îlot signale par l'homme de vigie
Est un Eldorado promis par le Destin;
L'Imagination qui dresse son orgie
Ne trouve qu'un récif aux clartés du matin.[2]

My lips moved repetitiously, mimicking each thrust of my oar — pulling me and my pain along with the boat.

Sweat soaked my cap, saturating it until its cloth could hold no more. A rivulet escaped and trickled down my temple, followed by a flood that rolled from the top of my head, down my brow, and poured into my eyes. The salt stung and I blinked furiously to clear my vision; to maintain eye contact with that spot on Wayne's shirt. The passing scenery — the banks of the Hayes River — was a blur of green and grey. I wondered how Baudelaire had fared on his long sea voyage to and from India in the 1840s.[3] I was sure he had travelled in far greater comfort than we, the York boat crew.

Beside me, to my left, Simon grinned and grunted with the exertion. Behind us, toward the front of the boat, five other rowers bent to the task. The York boat leapt forward, creating a sizeable bow wave. Ken looked steadfastly ahead. His eyes, hidden as usual behind dark glasses, betrayed no thoughts: the copper skin of his face an expressionless mask. Both of his hands firmly gripped the long steering sweep. In the canoe, close by our stern, but off to starboard a little, Charlie and Gordon kept pace with us, their outboard motor purring softly.

Charlie called out to the rowers in encouragement; his powerful voice driving us to greater effort. We responded and dug deeper, into ourselves, and with the oars. The physical efforts of the previous weeks had been worthwhile. The rowers worked as a team, concentrating on a steady rhythm. As long as I followed Wayne's fluid movements, I knew I could keep up with the others.

We all knew there were more rapids ahead, more dangers; more hard work. McKay's often-heard cries of tempo change, "Aha, boys!

Oho, boys!" were designed to break the tedium of long hours on the rowing benches, as well as to increase speed. Sudden spurts of acceleration tended to force the adrenaline through all our bodies, whether we were rowing or not. We would need that extra drive to negotiate the whitewater rapids and semi-submerged rocks still to come.

We were alone on the river. Our last contact with people was back at Robinson Portage, on the first night of that back-breaking overland traverse. Since then the river, the granite cliffs, and the forests of spruce, tamarack, and lobstick pine on either side, had been ours and ours alone. Briefly our passing touched both as we, twelve Cree, one outsider, a York boat, and a canoe rambled onward toward the sea.

Behind us stretched an invisible trail of defeated rapids. All, in some way or other, attempted to block our progress. Some almost succeeded, for a while. A few, wilder than others, tried to dash our expedition hopes and our boat on sharp-edged rocks. So far all had failed, though we and the boat bore the scars of each and every successive encounter. Our hands were cracked and blistered. Arms and legs bore multiple cuts and bruises. As they healed they were replaced by fresh slashes and new contusions. We were destined to earn many more superficial injuries in the next day or so.

Less than two weeks before, I was in Winnipeg studying York boats and their history, while nursing slowly mending broken ribs — the result of a fall in the Swiss Alps two weeks prior. Now, with a long oar clamped in both hands, I pulled with all my might, the injured ribs all but forgotten. My eyes focused on Wayne's shirt. My mind wandered away from Baudelaire, trying to recall half-forgotten lines from another poet's classic prose.

Pilgrim of life, follow you this pathway. Follow the path which the afternoon sun has trod.[4]

Rabindranath Tagore's words sounded lonely — as lonely as I sometimes felt on the river, although I was constantly surrounded by people. A pilgrim of life following a river the afternoon sun was already preparing to leave. My pathway flowed against the sun. My progress determined not by a celestial body, but subject to the whims of the Cree. Where they go, I go.

During those few days in Winnipeg, I spent many long hours curled up in my hotel room with books, historical articles, and my notepads. The rest was good for my ribs and beneficial to my mind. I studied for hours each day.

The Hudson's Bay Company (also referred to in this book as HBC), which controlled the Hayes River York boat and canoe freight route for over twenty decades, came into being in its earliest form in 1667 in London, England.[5] A syndicate of businessmen,[6] headed by Prince Rupert,[7] formed the Company of Adventurers with the intention of exploiting the reportedly fur-rich lands, and possible mineral wealth, to the west of Hudson Bay.[8]

Nonsuch,[9] the first vessel actively employed by the syndicate that would eventually become the Hudson's Bay Company, was no leviathan of the seas. Carrying a crew of only eleven men, she stretched no more than fifty-three feet on deck (sixteen metres), ignoring the lengthy bowsprit. That's only nine feet (2.75 metres) longer than the Norway House Cree York boat — an extremely small ship for the Atlantic crossing: little more than a cockleshell on the unpredictable and hazardous ice-choked waters of Hudson Strait and Hudson Bay. *Nonsuch* did not visit the Hayes River, or any other estuary or potential trading post site on the west side of the bay. Her exploratory voyage was intended to search for the Northwest Passage route to the South Seas and to trade with the Indians. Ice conditions in the northern half of the bay sent the small ship due south from Hudson Strait into James Bay, the large inlet at the foot of Hudson Bay. There, Captain Zachariah Gillam[10] and fur-trade guide Médart Chouart, Sieur des Groseilliers[11] established a trading post at the mouth of a river. The "house" they built, from logs caulked with moss, they named Charles Fort in honour of the English king.[12] They named the river after Prince Rupert.

When *Nonsuch* returned to England in the autumn of the following year, the *London Gazette* announced:[13]

> This last night came in here the "Nonsuch Ketch", which having endeavoured to make out a passage by the North-West, was in those seas environed with Ice, which opposing her progress, the men were forced to hale her on shoar and to provide against the ensueing cold of a long Winter; which ending they returned with a considerable quantity of Beaver, which made them some recompence for their cold confinement.

The fur-trading success of the *Nonsuch* voyage immediately boosted interest in the Hudson Bay region. Building up to a small fleet of sailing ships, over the next few years the Company erected more trading forts along the shores of James Bay and began to look farther afield.

Library and Archives Canada/1988-250-17.

The departure of the second colonist transport from York Fort to Rock Fort in 1821, en route to the Red River Settlement. Their journey would be uphill all the way.

In 1684, the Hudson's Bay Company built a new fort near the mouth of the Hayes River, on the west coast of the great bay. That first fort was badly placed. Being too close to the tidal surge of Hudson Bay, it suffered from spring flooding. Subsequent moves found the ideal location a few kilometres upriver. Named York Factory,[14] after the Duke of York, it grew in importance to become the Company's headquarters in North America. From humble beginnings it expanded into a sizeable town with a burgeoning population of Europeans. Beside the fort the indigenous Cree set up their own village.

Conditions at York Factory, for both Europeans and Natives, were less than ideal. The local Cree were just more experienced at living in the wilderness. Both groups suffered unbearably cold winters during which the river and the bay froze solid. Snow obliterated everything for months at a time. Game was scarce and the people, both European and Cree, went hungry. In contrast, when the short, damp summers finally warmed the land, the residents welcomed the temporary end of snow. Dense pods of beluga whales appeared in the estuary. Caribou herds roamed the mossy tundra. Ducks and geese returned from the south. A few black bears found their way to the coast and polar bears ambled in from the ice floes to help liven things up a little. The advent of summer also awakened the North's greatest pest. One York Factory resident complained that there were only two seasons at York: winter and mosquitoes.[15]

The fur trade was the prime reason for York Factory's presence and, indeed, for the Hudson's Bay Company's existence. That far-flung enterprise developed into an enormous organization. Through the wide-ranging explorations of the Company's employees in their search for ongoing trade, and the resultant economic development, the Hudson's Bay Company formed the backbone for the vast area of land that is now Canada. Even so, at the end of the eighteenth century, after being in existence for 133 years, the Company still had less than five hundred employees posted in North America. It did, however, have trading posts on James Bay, the west coast of

Hudson Bay, and far inland; wherever the mighty rivers took the Company's servants.[16]

The list of Hudson's Bay Company personnel in those decades reads today like an historical catalogue of explorers and exploration. In no particular order, the following adventurers were on the employee roster at varying stages in the Company's history. The list is a sample only and by no means complete, but most of these men would have known the Hayes River trade route well.

David Thompson[17] became famous as a cartographer. His early maps were of inestimable value in the modern mapping of western Canada. Pierre Radisson and his brother-in-law, Médard Chouart, Sieur des Groseilliers, both extremely capable wilderness adventurers, were involved in the creation of the Company. Dr. John Rae,[18] one-time chief factor of the Hudson's Bay Company, was certainly the greatest explorer to roam and map the northern Canadian wilderness. Henry Kelsey,[19] little more than a confident boy in his late teenage years on his first expedition, trekked inland from York Factory and spent two years exploring the prairies. Later he travelled to Hudson Bay to learn more of its northern limits. Aged explorer James Knight[20] was a Company man. His expedition of 1719, also to northern Hudson Bay, ended in mystery and tragedy. And then there was Samuel Hearne,[21] perhaps the best-known of them all. He would one day command Prince of Wales Fort, opposite present-day Churchill. Hearne undertook many spectacular journeys through the unknown tundra. Historian George J. Luste justifiably referred to Samuel Hearne as the "Marco Polo of the Barren Lands."[22]

Thanks to these intrepid men, and a host of others, the Hudson's Bay Company name became synonymous with the exploration of central and western Canada. For more than two hundred years the Company's servants, both European and Cree, ventured along raging, tumbling rivers in search of profit and, sometimes, each other. One of those rivers, the mighty Hayes, became the fur-trade highway to the immensity of the interior lands. In the late twentieth century, a modern band of Cree, plus one Anglo-Canadian, prepared themselves to challenge the most important river in the Hudson's Bay Company's history.

The Hayes River stretches for hundreds of kilometres across Manitoba, flowing in a northeasterly direction. It is one of the few untouched major rivers in Canada. There are no hydroelectric dams, and only two settlements along its route — Norway House and Oxford House. In June 2006, the Hayes finally received its long-overdue classification as a Canadian National Heritage River.[23] As such, it will be protected against incursion by commercial interests and joins a distinguished and growing list of more than forty great Canadian rivers now protected by the CHRS, Canada's national river conservation program.[24]

Unlike the fur traders of a bygone era, there were no riches waiting at the end of the river for us. No tightly packed bales of furs stowed in the boat to be sold or traded. No factor waiting at York Factory to greet us and check our cargo. We were just thirteen late-twentieth-century voyageurs heading down river in search of adventure and hoping for a glimpse into the past.

One afternoon, during my brief stay in Winnipeg, I visited Lower Fort Garry. This national historic park was the early headquarters and residence of the Hudson's Bay Company's governor, George Simpson, and his wife, Frances. George Simpson was a Scottish businessman who became one of the Hudson's Bay Company's most influential executives. A tireless traveller, Simpson came to know all the HBC fur-trade routes intimately, including the Hayes River.[25]

Three original York boats are on display there, two in the open, one under cover. The covered boat is claimed to be the last working York boat, sent to the fort from Norway House in 1935. Like Governor George Simpson, that boat had experienced the Hayes River in all its moods. I leaned against the weathered, dry, grey wood of an aged hull and tried to imagine what the open boat's voyages were like. With no cabin, or other form of shelter, rain would turn a hard journey into abject misery. The slightly raised stem and stern promised some protection from waves on the larger lakes. Otherwise, both crew and cargo were at the mercy of the elements.

Inside the museum, a well-arranged diorama showed, in words and pictures, some of the trials and tribulations faced by the early fur traders. Life for the York boat crews, especially on the long and often dangerous voyages between the Red River Settlement (present-day Winnipeg) and York Factory, had never been a picnic. I was soon to experience first-hand the beauty of the river's setting, the dangers of the rapids, and the extreme physical effort required on the portages.

From Lower Fort Garry I took a side trip to the open-air maritime museum at Selkirk. Among the preserved lake and river steamers and the restored Winnipeg yawls, was another York boat. Built in 1967 by the members of HMCS *Chippawa*[26] in Winnipeg as a Centennial project, the boat, although smaller, is almost identical in construction to Ken McKay's boat.

A voice calls for water, bringing my mind to the present. A tin mug is passed from one to another, filled with cool, refreshing river water to soothe a parched throat. I'm immediately thirsty — the power of suggestion — and reach for my own mug while trying to maintain rhythm with one hand.

I met Ken McKay and Charlie in Winnipeg. They had driven down from Norway House for supplies and to meet me. They had doubts as to whether an outsider could keep up, or would fit in. I had my own concerns, yet had no wish to be rejected. It was interview time. Would I pass muster? Over coffee in a hotel restaurant, we discussed the forthcoming adventure.

"I have a difficult name so you can call me Charlie Long Name for short," Charlie Muchikekwanape introduced himself with a smile and a flair that was to prove typical of his sense of humour and intelligence. In his mid-thirties, tall and solidly built, he sported

A traditional York boat at Lower Fort Garry near Winnipeg. Now weathered and grey, the boat is a perfect example of the Yorks that carried freight up and down the Hayes River.

York boats were Spartan — but spacious — and could carry considerably larger loads than even the biggest freight canoes.

a long, glistening, black ponytail tied back with a beaded thong. Ken, by contrast, was obviously closer to my age — though a few years younger. He was heavily built, with short, black, wavy hair. For an hour we discussed my background, the river, the York boat, and the book I planned to write. I had the impression that my many wilderness experiences in the Arctic, Africa, the Middle East, and elsewhere[27] failed to move them. Their interest in me was solely based on how I would fare in their wilderness. They studied me as acutely as I studied them. They wondered about me. I wondered about them. We would be living and working close together for the next few weeks.

A couple of days after meeting Ken and Charlie, I took an early-morning flight north over Lake Winnipeg to Norway House. Thick, threatening storm clouds were gathering along the southern edge of the lake, suggesting Winnipeg might be in for heavy rains. Thinking of the exposure in an open York boat, I hoped they would continue soaking the south and leave the north alone for a while longer.

We circled and climbed above the weather: the Perimeter Airlines pilot taking the prop-jet on the most comfortable route to our destination. Behind us, Winnipeg was lost to sight. Below us, Lake Winnipeg[28] — at 24,387 square kilometres (9,416 square miles) in area and one of the largest lakes in the world — looked like an ocean. Ahead, the forested lands of lakes and rivers on the Canadian Shield, where settlements are few and far between, reached to and beyond the horizon. Within an hour we skimmed low over Little Playgreen Lake, dropped below treetop height and settled gently on the runway at Norway House. The adventure was about to begin.

CHAPTER 2
The Historic Hayes

The Hayes River is the largest naturally flowing river in Manitoba, and drains the third largest watershed in the province. It begins its course near the head of Lake Winnipeg, flows north for 550 [*sic.* This is a typographical error. The river is closer to 650] kilometres through the vast wilderness of the Precambrian Shield and the Hudson Bay Lowlands, and empties into Hudson Bay. This seldom travelled river is characterized by remote stretches of white water, large lake systems, deep valleys and gorges and the unspoiled wilderness of the northern boreal forest.[1]

SO READS THE OPENING PARAGRAPH of a background study by the Canadian Heritage River System (CHRS) produced in 1987. Perhaps fortunately (and no doubt due to its remote location), the Hayes River is still rarely travelled in the early years of the twenty-first century. Certainly it is nowhere near as busy as it was in the

Map of Canada.

heady decades of the fur-trade era, 150 to 250 years ago. Manitoba Parks Branch recognized the importance of the Hayes River in 1983 when it designated it as a provincial recreation waterway.[2] Parks Canada had acknowledged the river's historic importance eleven years earlier.[3]

The Hayes River was named by French explorer and fur-trade entrepreneur Pierre Radisson[4] after Sir James Hayes,[5] a charter member of the Hudson's Bay Company and, at one time, the largest shareholder. He was also, in effect, the founding father of the Company. Sir James was the personal secretary to Prince Rupert, who had been instrumental in forming the Company of Adventurers, which became the Hudson's Bay Company. Hayes drafted the sailing instructions for the original *Nonsuch* voyage to Hudson Bay. He went on to become a deputy governor of the Hudson's Bay Company.

The Hayes has coursed through the Manitoban wilderness since the many glaciation periods of the extensive Pleistocene era.[6] Extending from the Precambrian Shield to the Hudson Bay Lowlands, the river's level is at its peak in May and June due to ice and snow melt in the spring.

Along its length, the Hayes is home to an impressive collection of wildlife, although, due to the densely forested nature of the river's banks along much of its upper reaches, many species are rarely seen by river travellers. Among the large land mammals reported in the region are moose (*Alces alces*), woodland caribou (*Rangifer tarandus caribou*), barren ground caribou (*Rangifer tarandus groenlandicus*), polar bear (*Ursus maritimus*), black bear (*Ursus americanus*), timber wolf (*Canis lupus*), wolverine (*Gulo gulo*), and lynx (*Lynx canadensis*). Smaller creatures are headed by the all-important beaver (*Castor canadensis*), Arctic fox (*Alopex lagopus*), red fox (*Vulpes vulpes*), hare (*Lepus americanus*), muskrat (*Ondonata zibethicus*), marten (*Martes americana*), fisher (*Martes pennanti*), white-footed deer mouse (*Peromyscus maniculatus*), mink (*Mustela vison*), and otter (*Lutra canadensis*).[7]

Perhaps due to the river's isolation, far removed from proximity to permanent human habitation (with the exception of Oxford House), three raptors are occasionally seen: bald eagle (*Haliaeetus leusocephalus*), the extremely rare golden eagle (*Aquila chrysaetos*), and osprey (*Panilion haliaeetus canadensis*).[8] Numerous waterfowl frequent various parts of the river, including tens of thousands of snow geese[9](*Anser caerulescens*), which use the Hudson Bay coastline between York Factory and the Manitoba–Ontario border as a breeding ground, and as a staging area during migrations.

Far beyond the last of the rapids, in sight of Hudson Bay, estimates suggest as many as two thousand beluga[10](*Delphinapteras leucas*) feed in the Hayes River estuary and the nearby Nelson River estuary during the ice-free season. In addition, harbour seals (*Phoca vitulina*) are common in the final few kilometres of the river before it flows into Hudson Bay. Two other species, ringed

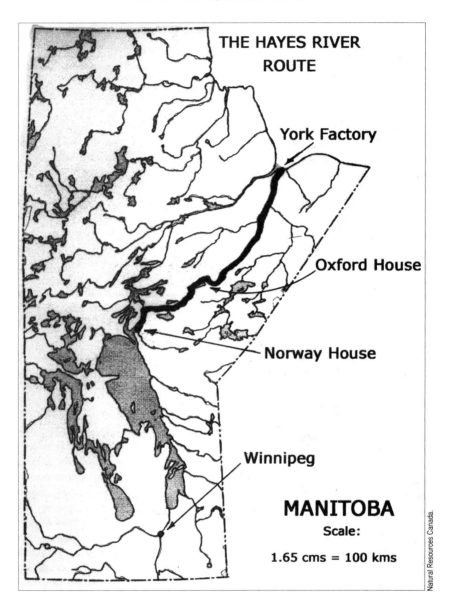

The Hayes River Route.

seal (*Phoca hispida*) and bearded seal (*Eragnathus barbatus*) are to be found in the estuary.

According to the CHRS report, the source of the Hayes River is at the confluence of the Echimamish and Molson rivers.[11] Royal Navy Midshipman Robert Hood,[12] a member of Lieutenant (later, Sir) John Franklin's[13] 1819–1921 overland expedition to the Arctic coast, referred to Painted Stone Portage as one of the Hayes's sources. Franklin agreed. He made comment on that portage site as, "… [It] may therefore be considered one of the smaller sources of the Hayes River."[14] Most modern maps, however, show the origin of the Hayes River to be Molson Lake to the south of Painted Stone Portage.

Over more than two centuries this river has watched a significant part of the history of Canada unfolding. It has done more — as a transportation highway it helped formulate the early economic value of this great land.

In terms of the fur trade, the Hayes River route from York Factory to Norway House can be confusing. Whereas we now know the complete route from York Factory to the eastern end of the Echimamish River as the Hayes, in the nineteenth century the nomenclature of the various segments of the river was quite different. The initial ninety kilometres upriver from York Factory was the Hayes River. It then forks into two: the eastern branch is the Shamattawa River (now God's River) and the western arm is the Steel River. The Hayes River route followed the Steel River until it also branched into two. The more westerly fork is the Fox River. The continuation of the Hayes route along the opposite branch was then known as Hill River until it joined Swampy Lake. At the western end of the lake, Jack River was a thirteen-kilometre link between Swampy Lake and Knee Lake. Between Knee Lake and Oxford Lake, the fur traders followed what they knew as the Trout River. From Oxford Lake to Painted Stone Portage the route once again became the Hayes River to some and the Jack River to others.[15]

In the summer, the river's flow varies from a snail's pace on the upper reaches, where the sluggish Echimamish meanders through vast fields of bulrushes, to long stretches of fast whitewater over the falls and down the rapids, and a still considerable current in the Hudson Bay lowlands. In winter, by contrast, most of the river freezes over, including the most dramatic falls and rapids in the harshest years. Toward the end of his first two years with the HBC, the young Scotsman, R.M. Ballantyne,[16] later to become a popular author of adventure books for boys, wrote of the river ice beginning to break up on May 18, 1843, at York Factory, after being frozen to a depth of six feet (1.83 metres) with ice for the previous eight months:

> The noble river …was entirely covered with huge blocks and jagged lumps of ice, rolling and dashing against each other in chaotic confusion, as the swelling floods heaved them up and swept them with irresistible force towards Hudson Bay….Where it was not so closely packed, a huge lump suddenly grounded on a shallow; and in a moment the rolling masses, which were hurrying towards the sea with the velocity of a cataract, were precipitated against it with a noise like thunder, and the tremendous pressure from above forcing block upon block with a loud hissing noise, raised, as if by magic, an icy castle in the air …"[17]

Ballantyne noted that the river mouth was choked with ice for a week, causing the water level to rise ten to fifteen feet (3.05 to 4.57 metres). It remained in that flooded state until, he wrote, "… About the end of May, the whole floated quietly out to sea …"[18]

With an average navigation season of no more than four months, between the beginning of June and the end of September, it was imperative that the heavily loaded brigades of York boats and canoes move as quickly up and down stream as possible.

With the spring break-up, as the ice flowed to the sea, it was followed by boats laden with furs from Norway House and farther west. Meanwhile, at York Factory, the residents eagerly awaited the news of the arrival of that year's first ship from England. Many of the immigrants carried on that vessel, and on the many ships that came after, would struggle up the Hayes River through a wilderness of trees to a new life in what is now Manitoba. Much of the cargo would follow, in freight canoes and in York boats.

In the summer of 1846, the normally peaceful Hayes River was disturbed by 347 soldiers, men of the Sixth Regiment of Foot[19] (later to be known as the Royal Warwickshire Regiment), and their artillery as they made their way upriver from York Factory to the Red River Settlement. Possible signs of that army's passing, in the shape of campsites, are still in evidence.

The Hayes River is a river for summer travel only. In winter it freezes over for most of its length. Few people have braved the wicked winter cold to experience its beauty once the temperatures plummeted to way below zero. But it has been done. The eminent nineteenth-century Canadian explorer and geologist J.B. Tyrrell is reported to have trekked up the length of the Hayes River from York Factory to Norway House in less than a month in the winter of 1893, mostly on snowshoes.[20]

I had flown over the Hayes one summer while en route to Churchill. I recalled seeing long stretches of obvious rapids and whitewater flanked on either side by endless vistas of green. In the summer of 1994, I was ready for a much closer look.

CHAPTER 3
Norway House

THERE WAS NO ONE TO meet me on arrival at Norway House, but I knew I wouldn't have to wait long for transport: I had been assured someone would collect me. Sure enough, after about fifteen minutes of kicking my heels, Irv Swanson, the economic development officer for the band, pulled up in a pickup truck followed by a cloud of dust to drive me to Ken's furniture workshop.

As we walked in, Charlie and a few of the crew were hard at work, smoothing and painting their oar blades. Supplies for the expedition were stacked haphazardly around the floor. Sawdust and wood shavings added to the general air of chaos. The scene was familiar to me. Most of my own expeditions had started the same way: one room of wherever I lived being strewn with apparently random mounds of supplies waiting to be loaded or shipped out. Irv made the introductions amid a hubbub of voices, all speaking in the Cree language. Hesitantly, perhaps shyly, the young men in the workshop put down their tools and greeted me one by one, each reaching out to shake my extended hand.

With the introductions out of the way, Albert Tait, a Métis who would not be going with us, sat on a chair in the middle of the room and told a crude joke about a parrot, a cord of wood, and a bald guy. I suspect it was told to see how I would react, in view of my own shiny pate. It was funny and I laughed loudly with the rest of them. Albert then said the joke was much funnier in Cree and told it again in his own language. If anything the guys all laughed even louder this time. I could only assume it really was funnier in Cree.

Ken McKay was nowhere to be seen and no one seemed to know where he was. The crew weren't doing much in the way of work so, as there didn't seem to be much point in my hanging around also doing nothing, Irv drove me to the small motel on the south side of the community. I checked in for one night, dumped my gear in the room, and went visiting.

Irv introduced me to the present manager of the department store, now called the Northern store.[1] That worthy showed me the old jail and original HBC buildings, both dating from the mid 1800s. The tiny, old, whitewashed jail, with its massively thick stone walls, had never contributed much to the history books. According to Norway House records, the jail only ever had one inmate. He, according to the story, was incarcerated for beating his wife. The old Hudson's Bay Company post, known locally as the Archway Warehouse, is pristine white with red-and-black trim. Close by is a full-size York boat replica on the lawns beside the Nelson River. A plaque leaning against the hull tells its own story:

> This York boat was built in 1974 by Norway House residents under the supervision of Charles Edward Campbell. Charlie modelled his own York boat after one he had seen in Lower Fort Garry and then returned to Norway House to teach others how to build York boats. Charlie chose to leave the legacy

© Anthony Dalton Collection.

The *C.E. Campbell* York boat on display at Norway House is named for Charlie Campbell, long-time HBC employee and boat-builder.

© Anthony Dalton Collection.

This original HBC storage building next to the Nelson River in Norway House dates from the early nineteenth century.

of York boat building with Ken McKay and the annual York boat races have evolved from this.

It was comforting to have physical evidence, at last, of Ken McKay's boat-building background. He obviously had benefited from a talented teacher. Even though I still hadn't seen the expedition York boat, I was confident she would be sturdy and hoped she would prove to be watertight. Charlie Campbell had, apparently, been inspired by the same York boats I had seen at Lower Fort Garry a few days before.

A plaque on a white-washed wall of the old HBC building also commemorates the celebrated Charlie Campbell who, it says, worked for the Hudson's Bay Company for forty-four years (1924–1968).

On the way back to Irv's office I saw Ken McKay's York boat for the first time, tucked into the reeds close to a house, which, I later learned, was Charlie's home. It certainly looked impressive with its mast and crosstree moving slightly in the breeze, giving it the appearance of being ready for anything.

Irv gave me a photocopy of a slim book on the history of Norway House,[2] and a dictionary[3] of Swampy Cree terms translated into English. Both items were extremely useful for my research and a thoughtful gesture, although the Cree language would not be easy to learn.

There are forty syllabic characters with twelve final consonants in Cree, whereas we who use the Roman orthography have but twenty-six characters in our alphabet. Cree syllabics, or *Pepipopa*,[4] were developed in the early nineteenth century by Methodist missionary James Evans[5] so that the Cree could read the scriptures. Anthropologist Alan McMillan[6] described syllabic writing as differing "from that using an alphabet by having one character for the whole syllable (minimally, a consonant and a vowel combination)." More recent epigraphers have suggested that the symbols used by Evans may have already been known in ancient times in Europe. Be

The stone monument to the Reverend James Evans, creator of the Cree syllabic dictionary, stands on Church Point in Norway House.

© Anthony Dalton Collection.

that as it may, James Evans was the man who taught the Cree to read and write in their own language. Eventually, due to his dedication and intelligence, the complete Holy Bible was translated into Cree.

There is no doubt that the Reverend Evans was a highly talented man and a dedicated linguist. During a long stint in Upper Canada he had worked with the Ojibway, even devising a written version of their language. He actually translated some of his own works into Ojibway for them. The hard-working missionary was also capable with his hands. While at York Factory he fashioned a canoe from sheets of tin. Evans is said to have covered thousands of miles in his shiny craft, making any en-route repairs with a soldering iron. Because it reflected sunlight and ripples on the water, the Cree called Evans's tin canoe the "Island of Light."[7] It is certain that Evans followed the route we were about to take, at times by Cree canoe, sometimes in his tin tub, and possibly by York boat. Evans and his family eventually went back to England, where he died of a heart attack not long after while lecturing to raise money for the missions. In 1955, over a century after his death, his ashes were finally returned to Norway House.[8] They rest, as perhaps they should, close to the lovely little white church on a grassy knoll. There, on Church Point, a monument celebrates his exemplary work and his life's achievements.

The Cree have lived and hunted in this area since sometime after their ancestors crossed the land bridge over the Bering Strait, between Alaska and Siberia. Being nomadic hunters and seasonal gatherers they travelled constantly in search of sustenance. The Cree settled in a vast land of forests, rivers, and lakes: a land where food was plentiful. They named each of those rivers and each of the lakes in their own language. They soon found all the best fishing spots, the most productive hunting grounds, and discovered the most comfortable places to set up their wigwams.

The land was different then; the Cree knew it belonged to the Great Spirit. The rivers were pure, the forests and plains rich in game. The Cree lived wherever they wished, though there were some potential restrictions. Their distant neighbours, the Chipewyan in the north and west were their enemies and to be avoided if at all possible. In the south, however, the Assiniboine were their friends.

Occasionally the Cree and the Assiniboine would join forces to hunt buffalo on the grasslands of the prairies. Sometimes the young men of the tribe went to war against the Sioux with the Assiniboine;[9] though most historians agree that, in general, the Cree have always been a peaceful nation.

When I was a boy at school in England, I was fascinated by all things associated with Canada, particularly its Native populations. Images of healthy braves riding furiously after stampeding buffalo were part of my childish introduction to Canada's history. Perhaps part of the attraction for me was due to a relative, my great-uncle, who roamed Canada in the early 1900s. He had lived in Moose Jaw, Saskatchewan, at a time when the prairie regions were still in the evolutionary stage between wilderness and farmland. I'm sure he must have had many opportunities to meet and learn about the Native Canadians. Sadly he died long before I was born. I would love to have heard his tales of adventure.

Raymond Beaumont, author of a brief history of Norway House, opened his work with: "Long before Norway House existed, there was only a river and a lake, part of a waterway that started in the mountains far to the west and ended at the great salt water sea to the north. All around, as far as the eye could see, stretched forest, marsh, and muskeg with patches of bare rock here and there. It was a place untouched by human hands."[10]

Standing alone on the shores of Playgreen Lake later that afternoon, with my back to the settlement, the Norway House area really did not look so different to me. I stood on a flat rock, bare except for some patches of lichen. There was still the river and the lake. We were surrounded by woodlands and I knew there were marshes and muskeg not far away. I could see why the early hunters and gatherers came to this place. It was an idyllic setting with game and fish in abundance.

In summer, the watery highway of the Hayes River system reached from Hudson Bay to this natural crossroads. The operational season, however, was too short for the fur traders in London. In the early nineteenth century, the Hudson's Bay Company made plans to build a winter road from the site of present-day Norway House to York Factory. Standing on the shores of Playgreen Lake that day, I was reminded of a tenuous link between me, the Hudson's Bay Company's ships, and the seasonal track.

On May 29, 1814, the HBC's *Prince of Wales*[11] set sail from the English port of Gravesend, on the Thames River, as *Nonsuch* had done 146 years before. She was bound across the north Atlantic, through the tidal turmoil of Hudson Strait, and into Hudson Bay. Her destination, as usual for many westbound Company ships, was York Factory. Eight Norwegians and one Swede joined the vessel before she slipped her moorings at Gravesend. The Norwegians had been hired to work at a variety of locations along the proposed winter road. The ninth member of the party, a Swedish naval officer, Lieutenant Enner Holte,[12] was the supervisor and interpreter.

One hundred and twenty-six years later, as the dreadful conflict in Europe escalated toward the Battle of Britain, I was born in an upstairs bedroom of a semi-detached house in Gravesend. Fifty-four years after that, I got ready to travel the river running through the land the Scandinavians had been sent to clear.

Prince of Wales, which was to carry Lieutenant John Franklin's overland expedition to York Factory five years later, dropped anchor at Five Fathom Hole on September 3, 1814. The anchorage, a few kilometres from York Factory, was as far as the ship could go. All the men and cargo were ferried ashore in company schooners and other smaller boats. Once the passengers were on shore, the HBC factor, or head man, issued Holte with his instructions and advised him of the plans. He and his party were to travel inland, up the Hayes River to the first specified site for the winter road. Being skilled with long-handled axes, the Norwegians were to clear up to sixty acres of land and plant potatoes. From there they were to move to White Falls, also known as Robinson Falls, fell the trees and plant rye.

The project was far from successful. On September 10, the Swede, the Norwegians, a Company clerk, and a handful of Irishmen left York Factory in two boats. At the end of the first day the Irishmen turned back for York Factory, apparently because they disliked eating pemmican,[13] and shipped out for the Emerald Isle.

The Swede and the Norwegians continued upriver. Holte had great difficulty in imposing his will on the unruly and hard-drinking Norwegians. The eight were difficult to handle. They fought with each other and they complained constantly about the food. By July the next year the troublesome team had only cleared about one acre of land on the initial site and erected two small buildings.

It was a start, nothing more. The site they cleared has become known, for obvious reasons, as Norway House. There is no record, or evidence, that the labourers ever did clear any land at White Falls. The winter road project had not progressed as planned. Canada would become a nation before an iron bridge spanned a rapid on a future winter road. Enner Holte, the Swedish naval officer, was destined for only a short sojourn in the new land: he was killed in May 1816 at Seven Oaks in a skirmish between Hudson's Bay Company personnel and the rival North West Company.[14]

Although its beginnings were inauspicious, for the next few years the population of Norway House gradually increased. Most residents were either employees of the Company or their families. When the Hudson's Bay Company and the North West Company put aside their differences in late 1820 and joined forces under the HBC[15] banner, Norway House began to come into its own. By the summer of 1821 it had become a major distribution centre for the now extremely powerful fur-trading giant. More than forty boats[16] (an estimated twenty-four York boats and thirteen canoes) came into Norway House from the west and south in June of that year, all heading for York Factory. Many more of each were to follow through July, August, and September.

Over the next decade, Norway House quickly grew in importance as a trans-shipment centre for the Company. Most of the original buildings were rebuilt in the mid 1830s and by 1843 the settlement was well established. In that year, Augustus Peers, a young HBC clerk, observed: "The fort, which is built of wood, is enclosed with high stockades. The houses are all of one storey high and being whitewashed present a very neat and pleasing appearance. In front is a green enclosure, intersected by platforms, the main one leading down to the river through the principal store."[17]

Norway House would maintain that comfortable appearance for over a century.

When I returned there was no one at the workshop and the door was padlocked, so I walked part of the shoreline near the old church. I whiled away some time by photographing the scenery and the orange and green lichen decorating the rocks lining Playgreen Lake. The early afternoon sun felt comfortably warm on my bare head. Its rays heated up a granite ledge beside the water where I stood. The flat rocks looked clean and inviting. For a while I stretched out on their warmth, thinking about the coming journey; absorbing the northern sun and listening to the water lapping against the shore.

Later, I sat silently in one of the church pews and thought about the forthcoming adventure. I'm not a particularly religious man but my thoughts felt similar to prayers.

In the middle of the afternoon I went back to see if anyone was at the workshop and to offer my help. I needed to get to know the men I would soon be travelling with. Outside, a couple of the Cree rowers painted their names in red on a white background on their individual oar blades. One smiled in recognition and the other said hello. I went inside and, finding a large broom in a corner, used it to sweep out the mix of dust and shavings in order to clean the building up a bit. Other oars were all over the place; lying on trestles inside, leaning against the eaves outside, and against a fence. There were a couple as yet unpainted. With the sweeping finished and the floor tidy, I painted the remaining oars.

As an outsider, at this stage, I didn't have an oar. Technically, I didn't need one. Once on the river, I was only expected to help out on the benches occasionally to spell one of the others. Looking back, the afternoon was really quite boring, but a useful introduction to the crew, the remainder of whom wandered in at intervals over the next hour. As with most expeditions, the mundane tasks to be done before, during, and after the project are as important as the adventure itself.

Ken breezed in soon after I arrived. He had a few words with Charlie, nodded a greeting to me, and went out again. Later, while I was helping tidy up, I found a heavy cardboard poster tube on Ken's desk. On close inspection I discovered it held tightly rolled maps. I pulled the thick roll out and flattened the topographical charts on the table. The up-to-date maps, on a scale of 1:250,000, covered the route we would be following all the way to York Factory. Maps are one of my passions. I studied the first part of our journey, mentally calculating the distances from one hazard to the next. There were numerous rapids and a couple of obvious long portages. I wondered how much experience the various individual members of the crew had behind them. Did they know how to read whitewater? Did they know how to run rapids safely? Had any of them ever attempted a task such as this before? Wayne came over and joined me. After a few minutes of watching me, he asked if I knew how to read the maps. I nodded and showed him the various geographical features along the Hayes River.

"That's good," he said and started a conversation in Cree with the others crew members. They smiled and nodded in understanding: the outsider could read maps. That was one piece of knowledge in my favour. None of them had much to say to me, however, their natural shyness being partly responsible. No one seemed to be sure what was going on or what the timetable was. It was generally felt that we would leave sometime the following day, probably in the early afternoon.

For a while I sat outside in the sun studying the maps one after the other, looking for major problems and making notes about possible portage routes. Later, having stowed the maps in their tube and replaced them on Ken's desk, I went for a walk in the nearby cemetery. It sits on a small hill behind Ken's expedition headquarters looking over Playgreen Lake.

Graveyards represent an important aspect of the history of a community, with the markers making for some interesting reading.

I was saddened by the number of infant deaths and concerned by the number of deaths due to drowning. Was it just chance that had caused so many able-bodied men to die while out on the rivers and lakes? Or was there some other reason? Most of the Cree know how to handle a small boat with paddle and outboard motor. Most of those I met knew how to swim: at least they could splash around close to shore. I suspected the problem was simply one of a lack of understanding of basic safety procedures. Many of the Cree go out in boats without taking a floatation cushion or a life jacket with them. I never did see a Cree wear one. When it was too late to do anything about it, I found we did not have anything remotely like a life jacket on the York boat.

A little later, Ken came back and announced a meeting of the crew that evening. I was not invited; not being officially part of the team. Charlie drove me back to the motel and promised to have me picked up in the morning. With much on my mind, I spent a thoughtful evening in solitude. For a couple of hours I walked alone along the banks of the Nelson River. Happy with my own company, having many solo wilderness journeys behind me, I was well content to spend time by myself. I am used to being alone in strange places. That long walk was, as far as I knew, the last such opportunity I would have for some weeks.

Stretched out on a hard single bed after my exercise, I tried to see into the future. I knew my own temperament and had no illusions about my strengths and weaknesses. With so many years of experience to draw from, there was little possibility of encountering insurmountable physical challenges in the days ahead. The biggest problem, as I saw it, was that I knew nothing about the individuals who would spend the next few weeks around me. Even their culture was strange to me.

I had to admit to myself, my knowledge of Canada's Native peoples was embarrassingly flimsy. I knew that our First Nations are the descendants of the diverse tribes who inhabited North America before the earliest Europeans arrived on the scene. That was, in effect, the extent of my general knowledge. My knowledge of the Cree in particular was limited to a few facts. I knew they were an Algonquian people and, as such, one of the largest Native language groups in Canada. In a mid-seventeenth-century Jesuit report, the Cree were spoken of as Kiristinon. Later they were also known as Kristinaux and other similar-sounding names by early Europeans venturing into the hinterland. Eventually the longer names became simplified to Cree.[18] A goal for the future would be to learn as much as I could about my adopted country's first inhabitants. For the moment, I needed to concentrate on the coming journey.

There were moments that evening in Norway House when I don't think I have ever felt less confident about my role in an expedition or adventure of any kind. My background role in the York boat expedition would be a completely new experience for me.

Sleep is a great cure for many ailments, mental as well as physical. In the morning I had a hot shower followed by a large, unhealthy breakfast of eggs, bacon, toast, and strong black coffee. Outside the day was cool and clear, with only a few puffy white clouds drifting across the deep blue sky.

Library and Archives Canada/c-001170.

Norway House from Swan River Rock in 1878. Four York boats are moored in front of the settlement.

As promised, I was collected and taken back to the base. Albert Tait was there again keeping everyone amused with his stories. Ken was nowhere to be seen. The radio in a corner was turned up loud, with many of the crew and a few other guys hanging around it. Someone called for quiet. For a few minutes we listened carefully while Ken was interviewed by a reporter, her clear, confident voice contrasting with Ken's nervous tones. He acquitted himself well enough and answered the questions in a reasonably professional manner. After a little prompting from the interviewer he even admitted there was one non-Cree among the expedition team, although he seemed to have trouble remembering my name and where I came from.

There was a mood of excitement all around. It looked as though the expedition was about to become a reality. Ken came back and rattled off a series of orders in Cree, none of which I understood. Albert offered to take me for a drive around the community, and finish up at the Northern store (a grocery store chain operated by the North West Company that caters to remote northern Canadian communities) where last-minute food purchases would be made. Ken's orders, I soon learned, were to help him get the food supplies.

As we roamed the narrow paved roads sheltered by trees, Albert talked of The Creator. Albert, who admits he used to be a powerful drinking man, (his words, not mine) is a thoughtful born-again Christian in his late thirties. He gave me a braid of sweetgrass[19] that he had woven for me the night before.

"Take this with you. It is sacred. It will keep you safe. And think of The Creator each day," he told me. I put the pleasantly scented braid in my pocket and hoped he was right. Thanks to Albert's kindness I felt a little more confidence in the coming adventure. To this day, that braid of sweetgrass hangs in the cabin of my sailboat within arm's reach of the chart table. Each time I see it I am reminded of Albert; his kindness to me and his wonderful sense of humour.

Albert told me the Métis, his people, are products of the fur-trade era. Sometimes rudely referred to as half-breeds, the Métis are

Geological Survey of Canada/Library and Archives Canada/PA-038283.

In 1819 Norway House was a tidy settlement surrounded by a palisade.

a relatively new people who sprang from the coming together of Native women — usually Cree, and the male fur traders — mostly French Canadian voyageurs, plus some Scots. In 1994, the year of the Norway House Hayes River York boat expedition, the Métis were still campaigning for their rights as status, or treaty, Indians.[20]

At the Northern store we loaded our supplies onto a couple of pickup trucks and took them to the dock. Tubs of lard, a couple of sides of bacon, scores of eggs, loaves of white bread, packages of wieners and hamburger patties, dozens of cans of soft drinks, and more, were all piled into the plastic ice chests. We wouldn't starve, but we certainly weren't planning to eat healthily for the next while.

Four of the crew departed in a small motorboat to tow the York boat from its mooring near Charlie's home. The rest of us began the task of moving mounds of equipment and food from the expedition warehouse and dumping them unceremoniously on the dock. When the York arrived, nearly an hour later, Wayne commented that they had had to bail a heck of a lot of water out of it and offered the opinion that a recent rainstorm was responsible. I hoped he was right.

Two men spread a large, blue, heavy-duty plastic tarpaulin in the boat. Big enough to fold over, it would serve to protect our personal baggage from water. Rain would be a potential problem in an open boat; the rivers and their associated dangers would create another form of damp. Other crew members sorted the food supplies properly in the ice chests and placed them in accessible positions in the boat. Two of the chests became foot rests for the rowers. Everything else was stowed under the bow and stern decks.

I asked about a tight roll of commercial firehose pushed far up under the stern deck. Everyone was too busy to answer me. I couldn't imagine what it was for. Without a pump it certainly wouldn't put out any fires.

A few kids watched as we loaded. Some older men came to sit and offer advice and encouragement. A canoe with an old battered outboard motor pulled up on the opposite side of the dock. That, I soon learned, was our support vessel. The expedition cook, Ken Ormand Sr., would be in charge of the canoe. Once on the river, Ken Ormand proved to be an excellent wilderness cook, even if he did use too many cholesterol-laden foods for my liking. Never did we go hungry under his culinary care.

Ben Paul, a quiet and shy man, came over and introduced himself. He was going home to Oxford House and had persuaded Ken McKay to let him travel in the canoe. He would help out with camp chores and assist on the portages. Later, when we got closer to Oxford House Reserve, his knowledge of the river would prove useful.

In total the expedition would number thirteen of us. Eight rowers on the York boat, plus Ken McKay on steering oar and John Wesley on bow watch. Ken Ormand and Ben would be in the canoe and I would switch between the two boats, depending on my photographic needs.

We took our places in the boats without any fanfare. With volunteer rowers at a couple of oars, we moved the York over to Church Point. A large crowd had gathered to see us off: friends, relatives, and the curious. Some stood and some sat on the grass. All were there to attend a short religious service on our behalf and to say goodbye. No doubt there were those who wondered if any of us would be seen again.

The rowers pulled the York and canoe close to the rocks and stepped ashore. With caps off and heads bowed, we listened to the minister's strong voice as he intoned the prayers. As discreetly as possible, I took a few photographs to record the solemn scene. Two guitarists tuned up and led us all in a couple of hymns, with enthusiastic help from the open-air congregation. The Lord's Prayer completed the service and the minister wished us a safe voyage.

As a final gesture, Charlie rolled our red square of sail out on the grass and invited the onlookers to sign their names with a black felt marker pen. Many did so while the others milled around, shaking hands with all of us. Quiet farewells were said by mothers, fathers, wives, sisters, brothers, and children. It was hard not to feel like a gate crasher at a private event. Even so, I was not ignored. Many people grasped my hand, patted me on the shoulder and wished me safe travels. Those few emotional moments as we prepared to embark would stay with us throughout our journey.

"Let's go, boys!" Ken McKay signalled our departure by boarding the York first. Behind him, the rowers took their assigned places. I seated myself on the foredeck and John Wesley joined me there. Ken Ormand and Ben moved off in the canoe.

Ken McKay, town councillor, furniture manufacturer, boat-builder, and adventurer, called out the words we would soon know so well:

"Aha, boys! Oho, boys! Come on, boys! Let's go, boys!"

The eight long oars dipped simultaneously into the lake, forcing us to back away from the shore. Ken swung the steering sweep to one side; the oars cut into the water again and the boat moved forward. The Norway House Cree Home Guards' York boat expedition, from Norway House to York Factory, was under way at last. The time was 1:40 p.m. on August 17, 1994. From the shore a voice came over a loud hailer on the roof of a truck, "Good luck, guys. You will be in our prayers each day."

For the first hour and twenty minutes there was little talk. The rowers, all well-practised after the recent York boat races on Playgreen Lake,[21] dropped into an easy rhythm. On the steering oar, Ken McKay beamed happily. His dream of many years — to re-enact a traditional York boat voyage from Norway House to York Factory, just as his forefathers had done so many times — was at last coming true.

Off to our right and slightly ahead, the canoe puttered along steadily. A motorboat, with the minister and another man on board, caught us up and prompted our first tea break of the expedition. Obviously there was no particular urgency on this day.

For the next stage I joined Ken Ormand and Ben in the canoe to take photographs of the York from a different perspective. She was a stirring sight. Many of the rowers wore sweatbands around their heads. With their black hair, quite long on some of them, dark skin, and solid builds they looked every inch a crew of traditional Cree York boat tripmen. Only their modern, casual clothes told a different story. As we couldn't see into the boat from our lowly position, they could just as easily have been carrying a load of furs for transshipment on Hudson's Bay Company ships to England.

Tripmen, the York boat crews of the last century, were so called because they were paid by the trip.[22] Normally they were paid half their wages at the beginning of the journey and the other half *if* they completed it alive. They rowed the boats. They portaged the freight and their York boats overland to avoid the worst of the rapids. They lowered the boats on handlines down some cascades and ran others with all on board. Unlike the tripmen of old, none of this crew was getting paid, before or after the voyage. Except for that difference, our experiences would reflect closely those of the long-dead heroes of this and other wilderness rivers in Canada.

The Cree, in particular the Swampy Cree, were considered by the HBC to be at least as reliable as their own European servants at hauling freight on the rivers.

"The Indian trippers invariably deliver their goods here in better condition than the Red River freemen," Governor Simpson reported.[23] Simpson acknowledged to the London office that the Natives were more honest than the Company's own European and Canadian servants. As a consequence of their reliability and credibility, the Norway House York Boat Brigade crews travelled without company officers.

"Indian trippers are by far the cheapest we can employ," claimed another Company man.[24] No doubt the last was especially true; although the Company did accept the obligation of partly feeding the tripmens' families while the men were on the rivers.

Flotillas of York boats, manned by Cree tripmen, frequently left Norway House in the summer months to make the downriver trip to York Factory. Those miniature armadas became known as the Hayes River Indian Brigades.[25] Travelling as a group gave them the opportunity of helping one another over the more difficult portages. The more manpower available to move a boat, the faster the job got done.

The Hayes River freight route had been in use, in some form or other, since at least the late seventeenth century. It wasn't until the 1820s, however, that the Hayes River Indian Brigades began to become a serious work force on the river. By 1865, when the freight traffic on the Hayes River was at its zenith, the Hudson's Bay Company employed 146 Indians (mostly Cree) from York Factory and Oxford House.[26] Norway House contributed a further forty-eight. Collectively they annually moved forty-eight York boat loads,[27] or a hefty 135 tons (137.16 metric tonnes), of freight from the remote post close to the shores of Hudson Bay to the waters of Lake Winnipeg.

On the first day of the 1994 expedition we travelled north down the Nelson River. Like the Hayes and the Churchill, the

Nelson also flows north and east to Hudson Bay. In fact, it joins the bay only a few kilometres north of the Hayes. It is, however, a much wider and shallower river that was never a serious contender for the busy transportation route from the bay to the Red River Settlement. The route had been tried, but was dropped in favour of the Hayes River.

Each of the three virtually parallel rivers flows over the ancient rock of the Precambrian Shield. Dating back to the Archeozoic period, the rock formations are well in excess of 1,300 million years old.[28] They were there when the first algae appeared; the first signs of life. And long before the first homo sapiens. We, the latest step in the human evolutionary chain, would travel where a relatively limited number of our kind had journeyed.

Global warming, regularly in the news today, is not a new phenomenon. Global warming ended each of the ice ages. As the land warmed up and the glaciers of the last ice age began to melt and retreat 11,500 years ago, a huge lake was formed. Stretching across Manitoba, from Hudson Bay to well south of the 49th parallel, and from central Saskatchewan deep into northern Ontario, Lake Agassiz[29] was once the largest glacial lake in North America. As the lake has slowly subsided and the land returned, the rivers have continued their uninterrupted flow. Those rivers have been carving and fashioning this track since the last ice age ended. Today, as always, they have the ultimate control over this route and its travellers.

Although we had left Norway House early in the afternoon, with only half a day in which to travel, we were confident of reaching beyond the first rapids before nightfall. Hour after hour the rowers kept their pace. Occasionally one would call for water and a tin mug was passed forward or back as the need arose. Drinking water was simply scooped from the river without stopping the boats. In fact, the only water we ever used came from the river or from the lake beside us.

For the initial thirty kilometres or so from Norway House the river is peaceful. The rowers settled in to an easy rhythm, driving the boat north on a smooth, wide waterway. At Sea River Falls the river's attitude changes dramatically. From one bank to the other, the Nelson River is nearly half a kilometre wide. Stretching the width of the river is a messy set of rapids running over a sharp ledge, and a wicked assortment of rocks staggered over varying horizontal distances. The total vertical drop is not much more than about three metres. It was still far more than the York boat could handle.

I was well aware that Sea River Falls was a dangerous rapid. A stone monument[30] in Norway House bears the inscription:"Erected by the Commissioned Officers of the Hudson's Bay Company In Memory of Horace Belanger, Chief Factor, who was drowned near here on the 1st October, 1892 and of Stanley Simpson, Clerk, who was drowned at the same time in trying to save the life of his master and friend."

That drowning took place at Sea River Falls when Belanger's canoe overturned.

CHAPTER 4
York Boats

J OSEPH CONRAD WROTE, "THE LOVE that is given to ships is profoundly different from the love men feel for every other work of their hands."[1]

The taciturn boat-builders born on the windy, almost treeless, Orkney Islands in the eighteenth and nineteenth centuries would, no doubt, have agreed with Conrad. Boat-building was a special skill. It was also a labour of love. The Orkney Islanders had learned well from their Viking ancestors. Some of them would carry those skills to the new world.

It is not certain exactly when the first York boat went into service in the North American wilderness. It is, however, well known that the earliest York boats were not used on the Hayes River system. Nor did they originate at York Factory.

An Orkneyman named Joseph Isbister[2] (pronounced Eyesbister), is credited with having had the foresight to design and build the first York boat in the first half of the eighteenth century. Isbister was the factor in charge at the Hudson's Bay Company post at Albany House, on James Bay. Perhaps tired of the limited strength and cargo-carrying capabilities of the freight canoes, Isbister wanted something much more durable.

His eventual creation owed a lot to the open fishing boats used by his kinsmen around the shores of the far-off Orkney Islands, north of Scotland's mainland. They in turn bear remarkable construction and design similarities to the Viking longboats of an earlier era.

Isbister's heavy wooden boats began work for the company sometime after 1745. For a long time they were simply known as "inland boats."[3] The term "York boat" came later when York Factory was their main port. By 1779, York boats were the regular means of transport on the Albany River and by 1790 they could be found as far away as the Assiniboine River, some five hundred kilometres west of the head of the Albany River. There is little doubt that many of those York boats had made the long journey far inland from Albany House.

Around 1795, York boats started hauling freight — furs primarily — downriver from Cumberland house to Norway House and York Factory. Their journeys took them along parts of the Saskatchewan and Nelson rivers and most of the Hayes. Compared to later models, the earliest York boats were quite small, possibly only half the size: certainly they were nowhere near the size of the great grey hulls decorating the lawns at Lower Fort Garry.

Ken McKay's newly built expedition York, a large boat, measured forty-four feet in length (13.4 metres), with a beam of ten feet (three metres). Fully loaded it still only had a draught of eighteen inches (forty-six centimetres).

When Ken McKay decided to build his boat, he didn't have far to look for suitable wood. The forests around Norway House have an abundance of spruce trees, the traditional wood used in York boat construction. Ken made good use of the forest's bounty. Almost the entire boat, including oars and sweeps, is made of spruce. The ribs are the only exception. They are of oak. They were steamed and bent to shape in a homemade steamer outside McKay's furniture factory in Norway House.

The hull is lapstrake construction with fastenings mainly of stainless-steel bolts and nuts. The caulking is hemp and silicone. In keeping with tradition, the hull is painted black with a red trim: Hudson's Bay Company's colours. The eight long oars and two steering sweeps are also red, to match the trim.

In a paper on the labour systems of the Hudson's Bay Company, 1821–1900, author Philip Goldring[4] has reproduced lists of materials required to build an inland, or York, boat. These include such details as the exact amount and size of nails required, and the amount of caulking material and tar needed. For example: forty-four cartons of varying size nails; sixty pounds (twenty-seven kilograms) of iron; ten to twenty pounds (five to ten kilograms) of oakum; thirty pounds (thirteen kilograms) of pitch; two gallons (eight litres) of tar. The list of wood required to build a York boat with a thirty-foot-long (9.14-metre) keel is extremely detailed in the document:

> 20 boards 18' [5.5 metres] long:
> 4 pieces 8" x 1" [20 x 2.5 centimetres]
> 5 pieces 9 1/2" x 1" [24 x 2.5 centimetres]
> 4 pieces 11 1/2" x 1" [29 x 2.5 centimetres]
> 1 piece 11 1/2" x 1 1/4" [29 x 4.4 centimetres]
> 6 pieces 12" x 3/4" [30. 5 x 2 centimetres]
> 22 boards 16' long:
> 6 pieces 11" x 1" [28 x 2.5 centimetres]
> 4 pieces 11 1/2" x 1" [29 x 2.52 centimetres]
> 6 pieces 11 1/2" x 1 1/8" [29 x 2.8 centimetres]
> 6 pieces 12" x 3/4" [30.5 x 2 centimetres]
> 2 boards 13' long [4 metres]: 11 1/2" x 1 1/2"
>   [33 x 3.8 centimetres]
>
> For Floor Timbers:
> 5 planks 16' [4.8 metres] long 8" x 2"
>   [20 x 5 centimetres]

1 plank 16' [4.8 metres] long 9" x 2"
  [22.8 x 5 centimetres]
1 plank 16' [4.8 metres] long 10" x 2"
  [25.4 x 5 centimetres]
2 planks 16' [4.8 metres] long 12" x 2"
  [30.5 x 5 centimetres]
2 planks 10' [3 metres] long 9 1/2" x 2"
  [24 x 5 centimetres]
1 plank 10' [3 metres] long 12" x 2"
  [30.5 x 5 centimetres]
1 piece hewn to 6" [15.2 centimetres wide] x 3"
  [7.6 centimetres thick] x 40' [12 metres long]
  sawn in two for gunwales.
1 board 24' [7.3 metres] long 8" x 1"
  [20.3 x 2.5 centimetres]
1 board 24' [7.3 metres] long 8" x 1 1/2"
  [20.3 x 3.8] (for keelson)
1 board 22' [6.7 metres] long 8" x 3/4"
  [20.3 x 1.9 centimetres] (for ceiling [decking?])
1 board 16' [4.8 metres] long 12" x 1 1/4"
  [30.5 x 3.2 centimetres] at one end and 1 1/2"
  [3.8 centimetres] at the other end for rudders.
1 board 16' [4.8 metres] long 12" x 1 1/8"
  [30.5 x 2.8 centimetres] for stern sheet wings.
3 boards 12' [3.6 metres] long 8" x 1"
  [20.3 x 2.5 centimetres] for stern sheets.
1 keel 30' [9 metres] long.

The list goes on to detail the sails and the rigging:

Sails: 18' [5.4 metres] high and 9 breadths of canvas,
single seam, require 54 yards [49 metres] canvas #7.
Plus 30 fathoms [approximately 54 metres] staple

rope 1 1/2" [3.8 centimetres] for bolt rope with sheets and tacks.

Rigging: 24 fathoms [approximately 44 metres] staple rope 1/2" [1.2 centimetres], fully sufficient for two shrouds. 2 fore and aft stays and 1 pair of halyards.

Mainlines, should not be more than 2/5 of a coil of 2 1/4" [5.7 centimetres]. Whaleline equal to 52 fathoms [approximately 95 metres], but in seasons of low water steersmen ask for half a coil, or 65 fathoms [approximately 119 metres]. Painter needs 6 to 8 fathoms [approximately 11 to 14 metres] staple rope 2" [5 centimetres].

It's not really surprising the lists were so detailed. The boats were built at the Company's forts and, one assumes, the factor had to account for each nail, every yard of sail cloth, and for each length of rope used.

There's a telling quote on the fur-trade era diorama at the Lower Fort Garry Museum near Winnipeg. Relating to construction materials, including those for boat building, it comments on the problems of two men cutting trees lengthwise with a double-handed planking saw: "Two angels could not saw their first log with one of these things without getting into a fight."

York boats were sturdily built; strong enough to withstand considerable daily abuse. Even so, the early York boat crews, or tripmen, declined to take their heavy vessels over the more difficult portages on the Hayes River. Rightly they recognized the overland crossing would not be good for their boats. For a while, canoes were still used to ferry goods between some sections of the river, noticeably from Oxford House to Gordon House, on the Rock Hill River.[5] The problems of portaging a boat weighing up to one tonne, and measuring anywhere from six metres to thirteen metres in length were immense. We would soon find that out for ourselves.

York boats were normally worked by up to eight oarsmen. The largest vessels, about the size of Ken McKay's boat, or even a little longer, could have held as many as fifteen men aboard. Unlike most rowing boats, the York's oarsmen rowed from the opposite side of the boat to their oar blades. This practice required staggering the crew left and right alternately along the sides of the boat. At the start of each stroke the men stood up, leaning with all their weight on the long oars to raise them up and back. As they forced the blades down, deep into the water, they slammed themselves back on the thwarts. The resultant noises: of the oars striking the water; of the oars leaving the water, and of the rowers smacking down on their seats, sounded like far-off thunder.

I have heard the repetitive drumming rhythm. On the Hayes I listened to it almost every day, sometimes all day. I have winced at

The steel thole pins on Ken McKay's York boat gradually wore down the oars. Traditional York boats had wooden thole pins, which also wore down as they wore down the oars.

© Anthony Dalton Collection.

the squealing and grinding of the wooden oars between the steel thole pins[6] for hour after hour until I thought my ears would go on strike. It's easy to understand why people on shore likened the noise to the coming of a distant storm.

Ken McKay's only major variation from the traditional layout of the York boats of old is in the rowing system. Ken has his rowers sit on the same side as their oar blades. Just in front of the steersman, facing him on his left, sits the lead rower. Behind him, in the next three rows seated side by side in twos, there are six rowers. The final rower sits alone, with his back to the foredeck, on the opposite side to the lead rower. The rowing effort for each oarsman is, therefore, less due to the lighter weight and shorter length of the oars.

We know the old method worked tolerably well. Ken McKay and his crew, in their turn, have had regular successes in the annual York Boat Days races at Norway House with their system. Both methods are efficient and effective. The traditional tempo of thirty strokes per minute was regularly maintained for hours at a time. Decades later, Ken's crew proved they could match their forefathers when called upon to do so.

Tripmen usually rowed for roughly two hours at a stretch, before taking a five- or ten-minute break for a smoke. They then continued for a further two hours, and so on. Consequently, the time they were rowing became known as "a pipe."[7] Unless they had to portage, the only times they went ashore during the day were for breakfast and for overnight camp. Lunch was eaten in the boat while on the move.

The size of a York boat was most often measured by the number of pieces of cargo it could carry, rather than by its length.[8] Each package of freight was measured at eighty pounds (thirty-six kilograms). York boats were therefore known as "sixty-piece" boats or "one-hundred-piece" boats, even "one-hundred-and-twenty piece" boats, depending on their capacity. A boat of one-hundred-and-twenty pieces carried 9,600 pounds (4,364 kilograms) of freight, plus at least eight rowers, one steersman, a lookout, and, at times, a passenger or two, in addition to its own weight: a substantial load to move. Those small hardy tripmen of the last century were — of necessity — powerful men.

One young lady, who had the fortunate experience of travelling in a York boat in the late 1800s, likened the York boat's passage to a giant bug walking across the water: an allusion to the great oars, lifting and lowering like a procession of well coordinated legs.[9] In the days to come I would understand and appreciate her description, I saw the effect so often from the canoe and occasionally from the riverbanks.

York boats made some surprisingly tough journeys in the one hundred years or more they were in regular use. The long haul from Norway House to York Factory and back, on behalf of the Hudson's Bay Company, was a major route — known as the "York Mainline."[10] A few made the rough voyage on Hudson Bay from Churchill to York Factory.[11] We know they voyaged across much of Rupert's Land, from what we now call northern Ontario, into Assiniboine country, in present-day Manitoba. They eventually went as far west as the foothills of the Rocky Mountains. Some were actually built at Rocky Mountain House[12] and travelled the North Saskatchewan River, via Edmonton, to Lake Winnipeg and on to Norway House. In the early- and mid-nineteenth century, York boats made the return trip from Red River to Fort Simpson on the great Mackenzie River; a round trip of 6,500 kilometres (4,000 miles).[13]

RCMP Inspector Denny LaNauze set out from Fort Norman, on the Mackenzie River, in a York boat in 1915.[14] He and his party were searching for two missing priests. LaNauze went up the Bear River to Great Bear Lake and crossed it to the mouth of the Dease River. All told, his York carried seven people, their baggage, some freight, and two canoes. Their long-distance quest resulted in the discovery that the priests had been murdered. The Mounties, as always, got their men.

Delving into York boat history, one comes across fascinating nuggets of information, particularly regarding the cargoes carried. The bells for Winnipeg's St. Boniface Cathedral, weighing three quarters of a tonne, were shipped across the Atlantic from Whitechapel, London, to York Factory.[15] They were delivered from there by York boat. Wheeled carriages and the first pianos, for the comfort and pleasure of the gentry and their ladies, arrived the same way. Cast-iron stoves, furniture, books, fine French wines — whatever was required by residents of the slowly burgeoning town on the Red River — all were delivered by York boats.[16]

It is even possible that the first billiards table to reach the Red River Settlement did so by York boat.[17] Portaging standard "pieces" and York boats was, and is, brutal work. On the Hayes River there were thirty-four portages. The idea of manhandling a piano over a long portage is frightening. The possible musical interludes would hardly be worth the sustained physical effort. By comparison,

Glenbow Museum Archives/NA-1598-1.

When travelling upstream against a strong current, tripmen used long poles to force their York boat ahead.

portaging a cumbersome billiard table is beyond comprehension. Military cannons, too, for the Royal Warwickshire Regiment, travelled up the Hayes River by York boat to Red River. Perhaps the most bizarre piece of cargo carried was a package of human remains, destined for a long odyssey from continent to continent on wild rivers and deep oceans.

John Rowand was chief factor for the Hudson's Bay Company at Fort Edmonton in 1854, and responsible for the enormous Saskatchewan District. In the spring of that year he set out to attend a factors' convention at Norway House, before continuing downriver to York Factory. During a stop in Fort Pitt, where his son, John, was in command, Rowand senior, whom HBC governor George Simpson once referred to as, "Of fiery disposition and as bold as a Lion ..." died of a heart attack while trying to stop a fight between two tripmen. The ebullient yet brave factor was initially buried at Fort Pitt, but later exhumed and prepared for travel to Montreal, where he was to be interred beside his father. This created an obvious problem: how to preserve a decomposing body for the long journey, which would take a few weeks. The solution was quite drastic. Rowand's mortal remains were boiled down until only the bones remained. They were then packaged and carried to the Red River Settlement by none other than his friend, Governor George Simpson. There, concerned that the package might get thrown away by superstitious boatmen, Simpson had Rowand's bones sent to Montreal by a monstrously circuitous route. First, they travelled down the Hayes River to York Factory. From there the gruesome package sailed to England before being transhipped back across the Atlantic to its final resting place in Montreal.[18]

Robert Ballantyne wrote of the difficulties incurred with two young buffalo. They were being transported from Norway House to York Factory by York boat; from there to be taken to England on the HBC ship *Prince Rupert*. Ballantyne said of the bison, "They were a couple of the wildest little wretches I ever saw, and were a source of great annoyance to the men during the voyage."[19]

Domestic cattle were regularly freighted across the west in that way, which must have added considerably to the tripmen's labours. Sharing a York boat with a couple of highly strung, probably terrified, half-wild calves would not be most peoples' idea of a pleasure cruise. Cattle, I remembered from my early years in the English countryside, have a nasty habit of voiding their bowels when under stress.

CHAPTER 5
Sea River Falls

THREE QUARTERS OF THE WAY across Sea River Falls on the Nelson River there is a small, rocky island with a few trees clinging desperately to its tenacious clumps of earth. The island separates the main flow from a tumultuous torrent rushing through a chute about ten metres wide. In capable hands, a canoe could be safely paddled down the main rapid, right beside the island's east rock. An expert could probably take one down the chute and survive. The York boat, however, was too big for the narrow channel on the main rapid. It would have to go down the chute on the west side of the island. Rowing it in that narrow maelstrom would be nearly impossible. We would have to track it, or handline, from the island. Every possible man would be needed on the ropes.

The canoe team set themselves up on the island well before the York arrived. Ken Ormand lit a fire, boiled water for tea, prepared a snack, and waited. I looked long and hard at the chute and the approach to it. Studying the rapids from left to right, I couldn't help wondering which route the doomed Belanger and Simpson had taken in 1892. Much of the river ran over shallow ledges, where our big boat could not go. The deep water channel lay close to the west bank. Handlining the boat from that shore would present its own problems. On the island, we were in the right place, but would have to be careful or there was a strong chance of losing the boat on the first day. A small crowd from Norway House had driven up on the road to Cross Lake and had gathered on the eastern shore to watch us win or lose. We had to win.

We waited for what seemed like an inordinately long time for the York to join us; so long in fact that Ken O. went back in the canoe to find them. There was no problem. They had just taken a different, longer, channel around an elongated island.

The big vessel came in sight, her mast and crosstree silhouetted like a giant crossbow. Her oars relentlessly ploughed through the water as she approached: the rowers expertly keeping time with one another. From a distance, she looked like an ancient galleon preparing to enter a sea battle. I could almost hear the timekeeper pounding out the rowers' rhythm on his skin drum.

Ken McKay's York slowly approaching the island at Sea River Falls on the Nelson River.

As they closed the shore, we indicated the best landing spot, beside the canoe. Murray threw me a line, which I made fast to a convenient rock. Charlie and Gordon, Ken McKay's younger brother, jumped ashore and went to look at the chute immediately. They were familiar with this hazard, having portaged canoes around it more than once.

Before we could line the York up with the chute we had to get her over a low ledge. Fully laden as she was, it proved impossible, which should have been obvious to all the crew. They struggled to lift her without success for about half an hour or more, before Charlie called for the boat to be unloaded.

Even empty it was still no simple task. The York weighed in at about one tonne and we were working in the water on slippery rocks. Despite the difficulties, over the ledge she had to go and, after much pushing and grunting, shoving, lifting and pulling, over she went. Holding her tight to the island, clear of the fast-flowing water, we ran four lines out on her right, or starboard side. Wayne's brother, Ryan, at twenty-two our youngest member, and Charlie went on board to handle the bow and stern steering oars.

A couple of onlookers from Norway House pushed off from the eastern bank in a small motorboat and crossed to the island to lend extra hands and muscle power on the lines. Their additional strength was a welcome blessing.

The York bobbed gently in an eddy as we spread ourselves out down the length of the chute with three men on each line. Our job was to keep her off the rock wall on the opposite side. We also had to try to slow her passage through the white-water turbulence. On board, Charlie and Ryan would attempt to keep her straight and fend her off the rocks on our side. The theory was fine. It didn't exactly work that way in practice.

As she was turned into the current, the awesome power of the torrent grabbed the boat and hurled her down the chute. Before the two men on board could react, a standing wave less than halfway down flicked her bow to the right and her stern to the left. For a

© Anthony Dalton Collection.

The main chute at Sea River Falls, to the right of the central island looking up stream, is a wild torrent with at least two standing waves. The York boat had to be handlined down the chute.

moment she was almost beam on to the waves and in danger of being rolled. Ryan, standing on the stern, was, for a brief second, close enough to risk a jump ashore to the opposite rock wall. He resisted the temptation, although he later admitted he had almost abandoned ship. Instead he stuck to his task and fended off the rocks with his oar and powerful young muscles.

The crew looking after the stern lines from the island held on valiantly and slowly got the boat straightened again. On the bow, standing with legs braced apart and knees slightly bent, without benefit of a lifeline or life jacket, Charlie struggled mightily with the forward steering oar. The York crashed through the tumult created by the final standing wave and then she was out of danger. Later I wrote in my journal "… And that was only the first one. Not the worst one!"

Helped by the line handlers, Ryan and Charlie manoeuvred their charge carefully out of the main flow; slowing her in the swirling eddies, where we could drag her back to a reasonably safe spot to reload and reboard. With so much happening at once, I didn't feel any pain from my ribs during the exercise. The ache started much later in the night.

Portaging the canoe and the rest of our gear was a noisy and lively exercise. Everyone was elated at our success on Sea River Falls and felt we could tackle anything in future. We would have to take what came anyway: our baptism in whitewater suggested we just might be ready.

With both boats loaded again and crews on board, we left the first hazard behind us. The canoe shot away from the island as Ken warned, "Sit still, Ben." The current and agitated water threw it around a bit but they made it safely to calmer water.

As the York eased away from the falls we realized the sun had set while we were working. Red highlights lit up the distant clouds, bathing us in a gentle, pink glow. In the half light of the northern summer we headed downriver to the road crossing, our last link with civilization for a while. A small open car and passenger ferry, hauled back and forth by a steel hawser, connects the road running between Norway House and Cross Lake, the next reserve to the north. This was the last point of contact for the people of Norway House with the expedition. Those who had driven out to watch our passage over the falls were able to steal a few more minutes with their crew members at the ferry crossing.

We lingered for half an hour or so, even putting up with the unwelcome attentions of a host of mosquitoes for a chance to be among other people for a few more minutes. After more good wishes from the roadside, we re-embarked. Darkness had fallen, biting insects were plentiful, and we were tired. It didn't matter. Our journey for the first day was almost over.

A short distance away, no more than one and a half kilometres or so, we stopped for the night at a wooden cabin, or bunkhouse, bearing the name "Sea Falls Wilderness Camp." There were enough bunk beds for all of us for one final night under a real roof. From that day on we would be camping.

Someone fired up a portable generator and we soon had lights. As it was after 10:00 p.m. we ate cold beans out of cans, with plain bread, and downed a mug of hot coffee each. Outside, the rain, which had been threatening for a while, pattered across the wooden roof. As we ate, the conversation was mostly about the falls we had so recently crossed and the many rapids still to come. Ken asked someone to get him the topographical maps.

Blank looks from a dozen faces gave a less than eloquent reply. None of the crew could remember seeing the maps loaded. Each had assumed someone else had taken the responsibility. The roll of all-important topographical maps had, it transpired, been left on Ken's desk back at Norway House. I was furious with myself for not having taken the initiative and stowed the maps in my bag. Unfortunately, there was no going back and no way at that juncture to get the maps sent on to us. We would have to do without them and read the river and the land ourselves. There was a basic road map of Manitoba on the kitchen wall, which showed the river and the lakes. There was no detail, but it was better than nothing. I asked Ken if it was okay for me to take it for reference. He looked over his shoulder at the map and nodded in agreement. I still have that map in my files: a tattered and torn, grease-stained visual reminder of the route we followed.

With the map spread out on the floor, I checked the distance covered that day, pleased to see we had at least thirty-three kilometres in our wake. After marking the first night's stop on the map with an X, I folded the map and put it away in my camera bag for safety. It was of no great help, but it was better than nothing. Once the noisy generator was finally turned off, or ran out of gas, we headed for our sleeping bags. The rowers quickly fell asleep. I found I had to stretch out on my right side to ease the throbbing of my ribs. Even so, I was soon drifting into oblivion, happy with the distance we had covered on our first day.

CHAPTER 6
The Meandering Echimamish

EVERYONE WAS UP BY 6:30 A.M. and greeted by a light rain singing on the roof and soaking wet ground outside. We ate a breakfast of hard-boiled eggs, bacon, and bannock, left over from yesterday's late-afternoon meal at the falls.

Bannock is a flatbread made from flour, baking powder, a little salt, lard, and water. In the bush, once the ingredients have been mixed, the dough is flattened into circular shapes about one-and-a-half centimetres thick. The round is then placed in a greased frying pan and held over a hot fire. As the bannock cooks it rises a little. Our cooks always tilted the frying pan at forty-five degrees or more to get the heat all over the bread. The finished product weighed heavily on my stomach, but it was certainly filling.

The mosquitoes came back as we loaded the boat. They were fighting fit, fierce, and hungry; the sooner we got back on the river the better.

Two kitchen chairs now were added to our cargo complement. "Borrowed" from the cabin, which is owned by the Norway House community, anyway, they were far from necessary on this adventure.

One was positioned on the stern deck for Ken McKay to sit on; the other went to the bow. They looked dreadful and showed up incongruously in my photographs. I wondered how long it would be before they were abandoned. Sooner rather than later, I hoped.

"Caps off, boys," Captain Ken called before boarding.

Ken Ormand said a short prayer for our safety on the river and for the safety of those we had left at home. By 8:40 a.m. the cabin was behind us. The rain continued for a while. Some of the rowers pulled plastic ponchos over their heads to keep dry, but soon found them a nuisance while handling oars. That was the first and only time they wore the rain gear. Riding in the canoe with Ken Ormand and Ben, I was treated to a short history lesson.

"That's All Night Stand," Ken pointed to a large open area on the west bank and explained that the York boats used to stop there for the night. The upriver crews going to Norway House would meet the downriver crews heading for York Factory and spend all night talking: passing on news and telling stories of the river.

Ten minutes after leaving the cabin, as the rain stopped, we turned off the wide Nelson River, passed High Rock, and entered a fast-flowing eastbound stream.[1] A few riffles kept us alert in the canoe. Once again Ken Ormand warned, "Sit still, Ben." In the middle of the canoe with camera in hand, I also stayed perfectly still. We cruised through effortlessly. Within three kilometres the stream branched into two distinct flows, each with its own peculiarities. One turned north, the other almost due east. They reconnected after a few kilometres and meandered roughly north and west until they once more became part of the Nelson River. We chose the eastern route and wandered with it as it passed a series of small islands before it, too, coursed off to the north. Within an hour, on this rarely travelled stretch, we passed a rock with an ancient Cree painting on it; we were watched nervously by loons, a pelican, ducks, a beaver, grey herons, and a few cormorants.

"In a couple of minutes you'll see the Moose's Arse," Ken Ormand told me, pointing ahead to the right. Sure enough, there was soon a rock formation rearing out of the river, which, from one angle, did look suspiciously like the nether regions of an enormous grey animal.

This is a beautiful wilderness land with large, healthy trees almost to the water's edge. For much of our voyage to Oxford House we were in sight of pines, poplars, tamarack, spruce, and willows. I felt good about the journey and enjoyed the scenery immensely. After mid-morning tea in a tiny clearing, I rejoined the York. While we thundered majestically along the offshoot of the Nelson River, the canoe went on alone and faster than we could travel. Their job was to scout far ahead: to follow the Echimamish River and cross Hairy Lake to find the continuation of the Echimamish. A secondary mission was to find a convenient site for lunch at the far end of the lake.

Soon after our stream turned north we left it and continued east on the Echimamish River, at that point a stream no wider than the span of the oars. It snaked through marshy mosquito-infested land, bordered by willows, for over eight kilometres before suddenly widening out into a lake. Some of the twists and turns made by the stream were so tight that Ken sent John Wesley, a scrappy little fifty-six-year-old, to the bow with a second steering oar to complement the stern sweep, just to get us around the bends. John churned the water and bottom silt to a rich mud, like a chocolate mousse, as he fought to swing the heavy bow through the turns. Ken added his weight from the stern. There was little the rowers could do to help at these times. Their oars were far too long to dip into the confined stream. Occasionally two or three of the crew would use their oars to push at the close in banks to maintain forward momentum, without much success.

Hairy Lake might have one of the most apt names in Canada. It is shallow, perhaps only about one metre deep on the course we followed, and is covered with a dense concentration of long, green bulrushes. With a good breeze blowing from the west, Charlie and Gordon hoisted the sail. The rowers shipped their oars and we all settled back in the sunshine. The sail arrangement was basic. The square of red cloth had been permanently attached to a yard. This was connected to the crosstree by two halyards run through metal eyes on the underside of the tree. When the sail was hoisted, the loose ends of the halyards were each tied off to a hook, one on each gunwale.[2] It was a simple layout, but it did work. Getting the sail down in a hurry would, however, almost certainly mean cutting the halyards with a knife.

Only five kilometres from one side to the other, the crossing of Hairy Lake under sail, hampered as we were by the multitude of bulrushes, took a little more than an hour. It was a pleasant and relaxing hour for all of us.

We didn't see the canoe until we were almost on it, the reeds were so thick. Only the thin plume of woodsmoke from Ben's fire guided us to shore. Much of the ground was rocky, but flat, most of it covered in slippery, wet moss. While looking for a reasonably dry place to sit, with two cameras around my neck and a plate of food in my hand, I slipped on a flat rock hidden by moss and fell heavily. Fortunately for me, I landed on softer ground, broke my fall with one hand, and managed to keep my lunch plate intact. I suffered only a few bruises and muddy clothes, plus some embarrassment.

That was my day for accidents. The Echimamish River is narrow and shallow. The bottom, for one long stretch, is littered with round boulders that just slid under our shallow stub of a keel, leaving very little clearance. Soon after passing the remnants of one of four man-made dams,[3] tiring of facing aft, I stood up to change my position on the foredeck, wishing to see where we were going for a change. Ken, at the stern, not looking in my direction, called for more effort. The rowers, with their backs to me, responded immediately with a strong pull. The York lurched forward, throwing me off balance, and overboard I went. I just managed to grab hold of the stem post with my right hand on the way. I held on, reached up with my left hand for additional purchase, and swung my legs up the starboard side of the boat. If I hadn't, I would have been keelhauled and ripped in two. My camera, on a strap round my neck, thumped hard against the hull.

Murray and Simon, hearing my yell of alarm, dropped their oars and dragged me back over the side to safety. I was soaked from the waist down, had ripped the skin off the heel of my right hand and had cuts and scrapes down both arms. Ken saw the trickles of blood and called out.

"You okay, Tony?"

"Yeah, I'm fine. Just a few cuts, nothing serious," I replied, breathing heavily. I didn't think it was worth mentioning the fire burning in my left side. I cleaned off the blood, stuck a couple of Band-Aids on my wrist and the heel of my hand, and vowed to be more careful in future. I was embarrassed again and felt really stupid, even though I was only partly to blame. I've spent enough time on boats to know better than to move around without checking first to see if it is safe. A few days later, Murray Balfour almost went overboard for the same reason. Wayne came close to experiencing a similar mishap before the week was out. Neither incident made me feel any better about my accident.

My sturdy Nikon camera looked intact, but only time would tell if it had suffered any serious damage. Strongly built and used to rough treatment from me, I didn't anticipate any problems.

In 1815, Thomas Thomas, who had recently been appointed governor of the Hudson's Bay Company's Northern Department based at York Factory, went on a survey of the complete Hayes River system.[4] He returned from that arduous two-thousand-kilometre round-trip journey with a sheaf of ideas and recommendations for upgrading the route. Thomas was of the opinion that the installation of two small locks on the Echimamish River would make it navigable by large boats. He was thinking in terms of barges; much bigger than the York boats.

Sensible though the idea was, it was never put into practice. Instead, the Echimamish remains a shallow, narrow river, most memorable for the dense bulrushes on either side and for the abundance of beaver dams along its length. As a wilderness river it is exceptionally beautiful. As a trade route or, in our case, an expedition route, it offers now, as it always has done, a major challenge to the progress of a large boat. The bulrushes along much of the Echimamish River were so thick that the crew rarely had room to use the oars as they were intended. Instead of dipping into water and pushing it away for propulsion, the oar blades — nearly five metres long — kept us moving by forcing the reeds aside. Both bow and stern steering oars had to be used constantly as the river meandered through the marshland.

I had the distinct impression that we were actually rowing a serpentine course along an exceedingly wide river. Shallow and slow-moving, the river had been taken over by the omnipresent bright green reeds, leaving no more than a glistening ribbon of open water. I took my turn at Murray's oar for a while on the starboard side, without being particularly effective. Rowing with a single long oar is not as easy as it looks. I found it painful on my ribs and, I must admit, difficult to match the rhythm the other lads had set up. When I tried rowing on the port side I found it relatively easy although, being considerably older, I tired sooner than the others.

As the afternoon became evening the mosquitoes found us. A few of their relatives had attacked earlier, proving more of a nuisance than anything else. The squadrons diving out of the darkening sky that night were vicious, dedicated, blood-sucking warriors. No one was immune to their needle-sharp proboscises.

I put on my mosquito-net hat, which protects my entire head, and passed around a strong bug repellent to the other guys. The only way to keep the pests at arm's length was to spray oneself completely — clothes included. Even then a kamikaze-like few managed to break through our defences. No "Divine Winds" there.[5] They were simply a bloody devilish torment. We had dinner in their company. They weren't invited, but they stayed, anyway. Almost in my ears, barred by a fine impenetrable mesh, they buzzed angrily. Our meal was, once again, cold beans taken straight from the can. Each time I lifted my net to sample a spoonful of beans a suicide squad would dash in, as well. Some got eaten — my rough justice — others tasted me. There was nowhere for us to go. The river was narrow; the banks covered in damp foliage. Mosquito heaven. A few of us crouched on a flat rock jutting into the water, where an unnamed creek flowed into the Echimamish. The others stayed on the boat. We all suffered.

After our hurried open-air dinner, Charlie and Ken Ormand went off in the canoe to find a suitable campsite. Wherever possible, McKay had planned to stop at traditional York boat crew camping locations. There was supposed to be one nearby, if only it could be found. The York, and its attendant swarm of mosquitoes, followed much more slowly.

Chapter 7
A Score of Beaver Dams

WE CROSSED THREE SMALL BEAVER dams without much trouble as we trailed some distance behind the canoe in the twilight. There was no need to get out and drag the boat over. A flurry of strokes from powerful yet weary arms gave enough momentum to bump over without stopping. We knew there had to be much more effective barriers ahead. Those little dams were to serve as a warning of what was to come the following day.

For today though, the journey was over. Charlie and Ken had found the old tripmen's camp. We jumped off the York into thick mud and waded through chest-high bulrushes to the bank. A grassy clearing, with only enough room for our tents, was to be home for one night. The drawback was, we had to share it with the mosquitoes.

The portable generator, which had made so much noise the night before, soon burst into life. A dozen light bulbs, which Charlie had strung from trees on both sides of the camp, flickered and blazed. Any creatures of the wild which had been within hunting distance departed for more serene fields. Modern man had invaded their territory with a vengeance.

It was a relief to be sheltered from the mosquitoes in the tent, but I didn't sleep well that night. The ground was hard and uncomfortable for me. My ribs hurt from falling overboard and I hadn't been camping for a long time. It was always the same for me on the first night outdoors — I suffered. A few more days had to pass before I settled into a relaxed and satisfying sleep. On the other side of the large tent I shared, Ken and Gordon snored gently and happily throughout the night.

A thick mist shrouded the river as we crawled sleepily from our tents at daybreak. Tendrils of grey hesitantly explored the river's banks. In the reeds the York, perfectly still, glistened with overnight moisture. All around it the mist lay heavy, giving the ghostly appearance of a boat floating on a cloud, until the sun broke through.

> ... *Aurora, daughter of the dawn,*
> *With rosy lustre purpled o'er the lawn ...*[1]

The surreal image was not to last long. A cacophony of hawking and spitting greeted the day, as it would for every day to follow. I mentally turned off the poetic view, and my hearing, while I stripped and packed the tent.

Having breakfast under such circumstances was not pleasant. It never changed. Each day started the same. Most mealtimes seemed to be a signal for throats and noses to be cleared as loudly and fluidly as possible. Breakfast was always the noisiest meal. I didn't like it. I had never got used to it during my years in Africa and the Middle East. I didn't get used to it on the Hayes River, but I had to put up with it.

Morning prayer was at 7:30, a good early start for a long, hard day. Though not very religious, finding the constraints of most religions unnecessary and the self-indulgent warlike attitudes of so many faiths barbaric, I found myself looking forward to Ken Ormand's daily prayer.

The Echimamish River is notorious for its beaver dams. There are big ones and small ones and some in between. Some are new and many are old. Few people, except occasional hunters and fishermen, have travelled this route since the York boat era. Those who have tried the Echimamish remember most of all the beaver dams. Each one was, and is, an obstacle to be overcome. Going around them is rarely a viable option. With a heavy York boat it would have been foolhardy even to attempt it, unless time was of no consequence.

The canoe team went on ahead to check out the obstructions. Their orders were to start clearing the top of the first dam that might impede our progress. We skimmed over a couple, hardly slowing in the process, bounced over another one by getting all the crew together on the foredeck to tip the balance; then we met a daunting barrier. Ahead of us, a high dam blocked our passage. Ken Ormand and Ben were at work clearing the top to get at and lower the middle section to make a potential ramp for us.

Ken McKay called for ramming speed. That's not what he actually said. Ken gave his order in Cree. I made a guess, translated it, and held on tight. Eight blades flashed, spray flew, bulrushes snapped, muscles bulged, grunts and groans echoed. The York raced for the dam, faster than we had ever managed to travel before. Once again I was reminded of an ancient galleon in an epic sea battle, bent on ramming a foe. Ken Ormand and Ben scattered. On the steering oar, Ken McKay aimed for the clearing the two had cut. We hit the dam hard and stopped dead. No one fell overboard.

"Back water!"

The order and the action were simultaneous. The York retreated twenty-five metres. We tried again with the same result. There was nothing for it but for all hands to go over the side and dig a deeper channel. We all got wet; we all got muddy. The crew dug out the sticks and stones and mud the beavers had so carefully positioned.

Slowly, the dam was lowered in the middle. This, of course, resulted in a fast-flowing stream of water cascading through the gap. The boat still had to go through it.

Charlie ran out four heavy ropes and a third of the workforce stumbled through the shoulder-high rushes, dragging the boat behind them. With much pulling from one end and pushing from the other, combined with mutual vocal encouragement and regular laughter, the loaded York slowly ground over the dam to a higher section of river. With the boat safe on the other side, we then rebuilt the dam to maintain the water level for the beavers and for ourselves. The dams seemed endless. Each time we passed a conical structure of slim tree trunks, the beaver's lodges, we knew there was another dam to negotiate.

Beavers build their dams and lodges following instinctive, but clearly defined construction practices.[2] They start by selecting trees growing close to water and gnawing through the lower trunks with their long, sharp teeth. The logs and branches are then floated into the required position and cemented together with mud. Rocks and stones are also rolled in to fill holes. The dams serve to maintain a strict water level, allowing underwater access to burrows in the riverbanks or to the beaver lodges. They also, by keeping a constant water level, offer deep water for the protection of the beavers from other land-based predators. Lodges often have several rooms, or chambers, built into an area of up to three metres in diameter. Once built, they are extremely sturdy, supporting the weight of a full-grown man without damage.

On one beaver dam we encountered, the only reasonably dry place to stand to work efficiently was a lodge placed beside it on a tight, narrow bend in the river. At one time most of the crew were standing on the lodge with no obvious ill effects to the lodge or the dam: a fine testimony to the beavers' architectural and construction skills.

The Cree call the beaver *amisk*, and beaver dams are *amiskowitum*.[3] Early in the fur-trade era, when the white men first began to find their way inland from the sea, the beaver fur was highly valued as a trade commodity. European hat makers were willing to pay well for the soft, silky pelts. The French and, later, the English, traded axes, knives, and other tools made of hard, durable metal for the furs. Far superior to anything the Cree had seen before, they enthusiastically haggled with the foreigners to own the wonderful new implements. Even more impressive were the "fire sticks" that could kill from far away. Far more expensive and valuable than the other trade goods, the Cree had to part with additional *amisk* furs to get the guns.[4] Once they realized the potential these new weapons had for hunting, and for defence against invaders, they did so willingly. The guns made killing so much easier. The new trade was, not surprisingly, hard on the beaver population bordering the Hayes River. Their numbers began to decline in proportion to the number of fur traders working the region.

William James Topley/Library and Archives Canada/PA-010608.

The beaver's fur was highly valued by European merchants. The meandering Echimamish River contains dozens of beaver dams and expansive lodges along its short length.

The beaver, whose fur was so important, became an effective unit of HBC currency. "Made Beaver,"[5] or MB, was the top-quality pelt of an adult beaver. MB became the Hudson's Bay Company's standard form of payment for goods and services. For ten MB a trapper could buy a rifle. For one MB he could get five pounds of shot or one-and-a-half pounds of gunpowder. All York boat crews working for the Hudson's Bay Company were paid in Made Beaver. Standard rates for a season per man were: seventy MB for a steersman, sixty-five MB for the man on the bow, and sixty MB for each of the rowers amidships. Sixty MB at that time equated to roughly £4.00.[6]

Such was the demand in Europe for prime beaver furs that, by the early 1800s, the intelligent creature was almost extinct in many areas, including the region around Norway House. There is no doubt that trapping, using the newly imported steel traps and the rifles, contributed greatly to the drop in population. The additional use of castoreum, an oily beaver secretion once used in medicine and perfume manufacture, almost sealed the beaver's fate. Somehow the species survived and seems to be building a healthy population again.

Late morning found us bow on to a difficult dam. Close inspection showed there were a series of thick dams. Each blocked one of a network of streams where the river had divided to pass around outcrops of slightly higher ground. Thick bushes covered the miniature islands and the solid dams bridged narrow gaps. The beavers had done their job well. There was little room for us to work effectively. The canoe team had chosen the only workable part of the complex for us to tackle. That dam was no more than two metres across, with thick bushes on either side. The York would have to go over or through the dam and through the narrow gap at the same time, with considerable effort on our part.

Ken McKay opted to make this a lunch stop to save time later on. It was an idyllic spot for a picnic. Carpets of pink and yellow wildflowers, decorated with fallen pine cones, covered the ground. Off to one side, where lunch would be served under the shade of pine trees, there was a small lake surrounded by stately pink fireweed. An old handmade picnic table and a few broken traps suggested this had been, at some time in the past, a trapper's campsite. He almost certainly had been after beaver.

While two men prepared lunch, the rest of us got down to the serious business of breaking open a beaver dam. There was not enough room for more than two at a time on one islet. On the other side, there was no room at all. Much of the work had to be done in knee-high water. It was inevitable that the York would get stuck halfway over the dam. It often did when conditions offered little room for manoeuvring.

With the York jammed and unable to be moved, Wayne and Charlie waded into the water on the up side of the dam, intending to pull the bow while we pushed and pulled from amidships and the stern. They couldn't have known it, but there was a deep hole right where they needed to stand. One minute they were up to their knees in water, the next only their surprised faces were visible. As with any accident, no matter how trivial, the Cree laughed uproariously, as did I. Once again we ran ropes out to tow the York the final few metres over the dam to deeper water.

The Echimamish is known by the Cree as "the river that flows both ways."[7] David Thompson, who explored this route in the late eighteenth century, called the river "Each away man's brook."[8] Nearly one hundred years later a man named Malcolm Mcleod spelled the name "Aitchemanus" and claimed it was the Native equivalent of "Each man his."[9] To me, the name appears to represent the option each river traveller has of finding his own way over or around the beaver dams.

Often, as we cruised noisily along the river, always heading roughly northeast, a beaver's head would pop up out of the river to stare in amazement at the strange contraption bearing down on it. One gave a brisk shake of its wet whiskers, perhaps to register surprise at the loud creatures on board, before diving for the safety of its underwater haven. Muskrats kept to the shores as we passed, with no apparent interest in our temporary invasion of their territory. Dragonflies, somewhat more adventurous due to their aerial dexterity, regularly hovered over us for a few seconds before dashing off on important business elsewhere. Ducks and loons either paddled out of harm's way, or took off in a splashing of wings and webbed feet to land far ahead of us, only to be disturbed again as we rumbled on our way.

The two guys in the canoe, while running far ahead of the York, spotted a black bear up on a ridge among the trees close to the end of the Echimamish. By the time we thundered by, the bear had sensibly disappeared.

In total that day we fought our way over seventeen beaver dams, the highest more than one metre above our approach level. With the final beaver dam behind us, the end of the Echimamish River was almost in sight. From a narrow stream, choked on both sides by millions of softly waving rushes, the river opened out as it entered a gorge. On either side, high granite ridges, studded with hardy spruce trees, determined the river's course for the final half kilometre.

The Echimamish ends abruptly in a small, narrow lake of suspiciously smelling stagnant water. Wayne held his nose and commented, "Phew. I wouldn't want to drink that." On the north side, opposite a granite cliff, there is a natural roadway of smooth stone leading through a cleft in the rocks.

"Painted Stone Portage," Charlie announced.

The York Boat Expedition,
Norway House to Oxford House

The Norway House Cree York boat crew rowing hard on the Nelson River.

The first big test. Charlie and Ryan take the York down the chute at Sea River Falls.

LEFT: Crew members break open a beaver dam to get the York through. Each dam then had to be rebuilt to maintain the water level.

BELOW: A large beaver lodge on the Echimamish. Some were big enough and strong enough for all the crew to stand on at one time.

Most beaver dams had to be broken open before the York could be dragged over to the next stretch of water.

In many places the meandering Echimamish River was too narrow to use oars effectively. Forward motion was often maintained by the steering sweep.

The York boat shrouded in a thin morning mist on the Echimamish River.

The York boat at the beginning of the Painted Stone Portage. Log rollers have been put in place to assist the boat across the granite.

The bright red square sail worked well when the wind blew from the right direction.

Arriving at the beginning of the long Robinson Portage. While some of the crew walked the traditional route looking at problems, others searched — unsuccessfully — for a shorter portage.

Despite the terrain, the boat had to cross the longest portage and that meant long hours of hard work for all members of the crew.

A constantly changing track of log rollers helped keep the York boat moving on straight sections of Robinson Portage.

A rusting axle and wheels; remnants of a form of carriage that was once used to haul boats over Robinson Portage.

A full-size York boat in the middle of a forest on Robinson Portage.

Near disaster at Hell Gates as the damaged York is jammed across the head of the rapids.

The crew soon became skilled at handlining the York boat down rapids.

CHAPTER 8
Painted Stone and Beyond

PAINTED STONE WAS TO BE our first attempt at portaging, or transporting, the York and our cargo from one body of water to another. We didn't count the major beaver dams as portages because the boat never totally left the water and it was never completely unloaded.

We reached Painted Stone at 6:10 p.m. After the enormous efforts of the day, dinner was the priority. Fried spam, beans, bannock, and tea: tasty, hot, and filling for complaining stomachs. Once we had eaten, Ken McKay was eager to get back to work. He wanted to get the York across the portage that night. In his haste he, with our help, tried to take it over without unloading it. The lessons of Sea River Falls had not yet been learned properly.

We cut log rollers and laid them down to ease the boat's passage up the slight incline. Even with their help, we couldn't even get her more than a couple of metres out of the water. We broke two ratchet "come-alongs" (hand winches) in the process and burned our hands heaving on ropes. For two hours or more we strained in vain. She wouldn't budge. Gordon finally took the initiative. He climbed on board and started tossing our baggage at us. Everything movable came off, including the oars. Empty and weighing half as much as before, the boat slid up and over the incline on her log wheels in less than half an hour.

Getting her through the narrow rock cleft on the far side caused a little concern: the boat rolled too fast down the slight incline and almost got away from us. A couple of the Cree were close to being crushed between the rock and another hard place, the boat's sturdy hull. The creek on the other side, that's all it is — nothing more than a creek — was but a fraction wider than the York. We ran a mooring line from the sternpost to a tree to ensure she stayed where she was for the night. Not that there was much likelihood of her going anywhere.

By the time we crawled into our sleeping bags on the hard granite we were all exhausted. Comfort was relatively unimportant. We wanted nothing other than sleep. I wrote in my journal, "I feel very old tonight. Every part of me aches with a fury, my ribs more than anything."

In the morning I roughly measured the portage and found it to be approximately eighteen metres across and one-and-a-half metres in height. (Franklin estimated it at considerably less. He said it was "ten to twelve yards across."[1]) The apex was almost exactly in the middle and well defined. Although Painted Stone was a traditional York boat stopping point, we had planned to be at a different site nearly twenty kilometres farther along the river before camping that night. In view of the many delays at the beaver dams and the time wasted at the portage, I thought we had done rather well on the previous day.

The portage is named "Painted Stone" because there is, or was, a Native painting on the rocks. We looked for it, not particularly seriously, but didn't find any form of art, ancient or modern. Weeks later, after reading Franklin's *Journey to the Polar Sea* again, I understood why. He wrote, "It is said that there was formerly a stone placed near the centre of this portage on which figures were annually traced and offerings deposited by the Indians, but the stone has been removed many years, and the spot has ceased to be held in veneration."[2]

Governor Thomas, as part of his recommendations for upgrading the river route to York Factory, suggested the construction of a fleet of decked barges of up to twenty tons[3] (20.32 metric tonnes). One such vessel would service Norway House to Sea River Falls. Another would look after the next portion of the Nelson and along the Echimamish River through the planned locks, to Painted Stone Portage. A third would continue across Robinson Lake to the long portage past White Falls, or Robinson Falls, as they have become known. The rationale for his ambitious plan was that more goods could be carried per trip, and goods were easier to portage than boats. Having experienced the first couple of portages, we would find no argument with that fact.

In the low countries of continental Europe, and in Britain, river locks have long been and are still used to control water levels. Thousands of inland freight barges and passenger sightseeing boats annually make long journeys from country to country, especially in Belgium, the Netherlands, and Germany, without ever going on the sea. Governor Thomas was well on the right track with his recommendations for the Hayes River. Had his suggestions been adopted, the Hayes River might have had a considerably longer life as an important seasonal trade route for Manitoba and for Canada. The major rapids, however, would still have caused problems.

Midshipman Robert Hood,[4] who was with Lieutenant John Franklin on his first northern expedition, which came through here in 1819, referred to Painted Stone as one of the sources of the Hayes River and the source of the Echimamish. The surrounding rocky hillsides, with an elevation of 244 metres, are perfectly capable of shedding enough moisture to spawn both the Hayes and the Echimamish Rivers.

Lieutenant (later Sir) John Franklin travelled up the Hayes River in 1819 en route to the Arctic to search for a link to connect known parts of the Northwest Passage. Franklin and all his men died on a later expedition when his two ships became trapped in heavy ice while attempting to navigate the passage from east to west in 1845–46.

Perhaps in an abortive effort to save time, Franklin and his men tried to drag their much smaller York boat over shoals without unloading.[5] Time had obviously not improved man's ability to weigh up the options. They, it seems, had no more success with the experiment than we did.

Hood tells of meeting two canoes at Painted Stone,[6] which had left York Factory, without freight, two weeks after the Franklin expedition. They had taken just ten days for the upriver trip as opposed to twenty-four days for the cumbersome exploration party. Travelling by York boat, probably half the length of ours, Franklin is said to have averaged only about two miles (3.2 kilometres) each day,[7] taking almost a month to reach Lake Winnipeg — but he and his men were travelling upstream against the rapids and the current.

A day or two in front of the Franklin group was a boatload of Selkirk settlers,[8] men and women, almost certainly in a York boat. They had voyaged across the Atlantic in the HBC's fully-rigged three-masted 245-ton (248.92-metric-tonne) sailing ship *Eddystone*, which had travelled in convoy with the considerably larger *Prince of Wales* — the ship carrying Franklin and his party. One wonders which part of the journey was the easiest for them, the ocean crossing in a small sailing ship with no possibility of going ashore for weeks, or the rough tough scramble up the Hayes River to Lake Winnipeg.

William Sinclair, the former chief trader at Oxford House, is reputed to have taken a little over ten days to speed downriver from what is now Norway House to York Factory in June 1813.[9] A fast trip, indeed; one we were not likely to emulate.

We finally pulled away from Painted Stone at 8:55 a.m. Ken squirmed the York through the narrow cut among the rushes to open water. According to the topographic map I studied later, we were on the Hayes River when we left Painted Stone. Most sources I researched agreed on that location as the start. Midshipman Hood, who is credited with the first accurate survey of the Hayes River, certainly claimed it as such.

The Cree disagreed. They stated the Hayes River flows out of Molson Lake — thirteen kilometres to the south as the crow flies. Many maps, particularly those with limited detail, lend weight to the Cree's belief. However, that river, flowing into the Hayes from Molson Lake, is named Molson River on at least one whitewater river chart.

Soon after we left Painted Stone a float plane flew overhead, circled, and came back for a landing. No more than thirty minutes after we started we stopped for a tea break and a chat. Sociable though it was, I couldn't help feeling the stop was a dreadful waste of time and good travelling weather. It did, however, serve one useful purpose. I was able to spend the short break studying an aviation navigation chart of the area.

The newcomers, all three from Norway House, seemed surprised we had got so far. I gathered from the conversation that they and others from the community would be watching out for us from the air whenever business took them in our direction. It was a comforting thought. The aerial visitors also insisted the Hayes River flowed out of Molson Lake.

After the tea break, the Mid Manitoba Air Cessna took off from the river beside us, sending a blast of cold air over the York. The pilot banked to the left, waggled his wings, and turned back to Norway House. At 11:22 we came to the junction with another river.

"The Hayes, Tony," Ken called out. Just as our recent visitors had claimed; they all said it was the point where we joined the Hayes River. To this day, like Hood 175 years before us, I prefer to believe we were on the Hayes when we left Painted Stone.

The York, which must have looked every bit a traditional craft from the air, now passed through a wide granite canyon topped by elegant pines. Steep grey walls reared out of the river on both sides, climbing skyward. Fortunately the river was deep and sluggish at that point, allowing us to drift peacefully through. Had there been whitewater, the canyon would have been exceptionally dangerous for us.

Half an hour after the rivers met we scraped through a marshland of rushes into Robinson Lake. It looked like another Hairy Lake at first, without quite so many waving reeds. The wind was once again in our favour, blowing a steady breeze from directly astern. In came the oars. Up went the sail, and everyone relaxed; the rowers taking a well-earned break for a while.

Edward Monias adjusted his horn-rimmed spectacles, pulled his hat over his eyes, and settled down on the baggage out of the wind. Charlie, who rarely rested for long, was soon bailing out the aft section. Ken McKay had a wash. Gordon made up a couple of litres of fruit juice from packets of crystals. Murray pulled a foot pump out of a bag and blew up his air mattress. He was, I believe, the only one on board who had bothered to take such an item of doubtful comfort. Ryan took the steering oar while the rest of the guys dozed. By the time we reached the narrows, about one-third of the way along the lake, inactivity had been rejected in favour of sport. Two of the crew assembled fishing rods and lines and a spirited competition ensued. Great shouts of laughter greeted each successive northern pike as it was hoisted aloft, deemed too small to be of use, and returned to grow to acceptable size.

Ken Ormand and Ben joined us, tied the canoe alongside and came on board. Those two culinary treasures had a kettle of hot tea, plus spam and bannock sandwiches for our lunch. The air was warm, the wind only a little chill when it gusted. The sky was overcast, the sun breaking through occasionally. There was much laughter on board as the exuberant crew told jokes and, in a friendly way, made fun of each other's failings.

The sense of urgency I had experienced earlier that day dissipated in the pleasure of that short energy-building cruise. As we drifted with the light breeze, some fished while others whiled away the time by manufacturing tumplines for the next phase of the journey. At last I learned what the firehose was for. The guys cut it into lengths, about the span of their arms. At each end they cut a hole and tied a strong thin cord to it. The firehose became tumplines, or head bands, to help carry heavy loads.

I went out in the canoe with Ken Ormand to take photographs of the York under sail.

"You look like refugees from a Third World nation," I called.

"Couldn't be," replied Charlie, his voice ringing across the water. "We are the First Nation."

Forty minutes short of the lake's end the wind picked up and changed direction, catching us almost on the beam. We hauled the sail down and resumed rowing. We were close to our next portage at that point and gradually turning into the wind.

Where Robinson Lake narrows, the Hayes River funnels off to the north to crash over a series of waterfalls and rapids. The canoe, some distance in front, turned out of our sight. We heard a shot and later learned that Ken had shot a duck. Intended for a meal, it unfortunately was forgotten in the bottom of the canoe, with a duck shot the day before, until they both rotted and had to be thrown away.

In the past, Cree hunters only killed for food.[10] Always they thanked the animals they killed and offered them tobacco. Primarily a form of respect to larger animals, bears and moose in particular, smaller creatures were not excluded from the ritual. Without thanks for its sacrifice and without the offering of a gift, the creature might be offended and never be caught again. The spirits of those two hapless mallards were sure to warn other ducks not to let themselves be shot.

Robinson Falls is not the sort of place to attempt handlining any kind of boat. There is a main waterfall of tremendous power, followed by two lesser falls. The total drop is in the order of seventeen metres, with the initial fall being the highest and the most turbulent.

Lieutenant John Franklin fell into the river between two of the lower falls and survived,[11] although he did drift some way with the current and was in extreme danger of drowning. While bobbing helplessly, close to the rocky shore in shoulder-high water, his men were able to pull their fully dressed leader to safety. His dignity, one suspects, must have been severely bruised by the occasion.

It is interesting to note that, at the time of his impromptu swim, Franklin was suffering from whooping cough. The dunking probably didn't help that condition much. He did, however, have a physician in his party. Dr. Richardson,[12] who was to achieve his own fame in the Barren Lands and the Canadian Arctic, was one of four Europeans accompanying Franklin. The others were Midshipman Robert Hood, Midshipman George Back,[13] and seaman John Hepburn.[14] The names of their Native York boat crew members, without whom the journey would have taken longer and been far more difficult, do not appear to have survived.

Franklin's expedition portaged their cargoes and vessels in one full day. They carried the cargoes along the accepted trail, but dragged the boats over the rocks beside the falls, the most direct route. Franklin wrote: "I shall long remember the rude and characteristic wildness of the scenery which surrounded these falls; rocks piled on rocks hung in rude and shapeless masses over the agitated torrents which swept their bases …"[15]

Even though Franklin's group were going upstream, and we were going down, therefore assisted by gravity, our full-size York boat would not be so easy to portage.

CHAPTER 9
The Longest Portage

AT 3:30 P.M. ON AUGUST 20 we disembarked at the beginning of Robinson Portage. The thunder of nearby waterfalls echoed off granite canyon walls. From this point on, the Hayes is a river in an almost perpetual hurry and it doesn't slow down until it pours its soul into Hudson Bay. Before we could sample the river's speed, however, we would have to sweat buckets on the longest portage.

I wandered away from the trail, clambering over rocks and fallen trees to look at the turbulence. On the north side the river is diverted by a sheer rock wall. In a short distance, it drops about thirteen metres to the lowest level; then falls another four metres. On the south side, where I stood, it is channelled by boulders and fractured granite overlain with dead trees. It was not remotely possible to lower our heavy York safely down that torrent.

I went back, retracing my route over fire-blackened trees littered like burned matchsticks across a meadow of delicate pink fireweed. It was hard going climbing through the mammoth wooden puzzle of black-lined triangles. I noted in my journal that, "The forest fire which laid waste to this woodland must have been a terrifying sight."

Midshipman Robert Hood wrote of that same forest while on the Franklin expedition. He also saw the ground covered "with the ruins of several generations' [of trees]."[1] He wrote that he found the jigsaw of tree trunks so confusing as to prevent the eye from discerning individual trees. One hundred and seventy-five years later, had he been able, he would have recognized little difference.

At the boat I told Ken and Charlie what I had seen. Ken grunted and pointed at the faint trail in front of us.

"That's the way."

Ken and the crew were busy dragging the York out of the river on a cradle of log rollers. On the first patch of reasonably solid ground, a flimsy-looking trailer had been assembled, the wheels and axles having been part of our cargo. I didn't think it looked strong enough to carry the York over a smooth road, but I kept that thought to myself.

Ken McKay's York boat arriving at Robinson Portage. From here it is an overland trek of well over one kilometre, through a forest on undulating terrain, to pass the waterfalls. It took fifty-two-and-a-half hours to get this boat across the portage.

While most of the crew prepared to run the boat off the logs onto the trailer and then to dry land, Charlie walked back to look at the falls with me. Murray joined us with his video camera to record the scene. After a few minutes' study we saw there was a way down on the south side: a difficult and dangerous way, but a way nonetheless. It was a sub-stream, only a little wider than the York boat in some places, narrower in others, dropping through a miniature canyon. The York was much too big to travel down the stream, however, the rims of the miniature canyon could have been used as supports.

Charlie and I discussed dropping a series of dead trees across the rocks to use as rollers and using them to lower the boat. It was remotely possible, but we both knew it would be a hell of a risk. If the boat got away from us the expedition would end right there. Another hazard was the possibility of someone falling in the river and being washed over one of the falls, as had happened to Franklin. Although this was probably the route Franklin's expedition had taken with their boats, up the rim of the narrow canyon, I doubted that anyone had ever taken a full-size York boat up or down that primitive natural escalator.

We discussed winching the boat out and using a combination of trees as anchors and ropes as winch-lines. A few paces away, the current at the head of the falls raced past our position. Fighting it with the heavy boat was a daunting prospect. Close by, the Hayes River thundered unceasingly over the falls. We were almost shouting at each other to make ourselves heard. With my mouth close to Charlie's ear, I bellowed negative thoughts about hauling out at that location. Charlie pursed his lips and nodded his agreement. Without another word, he turned back. The longest portage was our only choice.

Our old friend Governor Thomas had hoped to see a road built over this portage.[2] The idea was not to facilitate hauling large boats; rather to allow their cargoes to be transported on wheeled vehicles

Robert Bell/Library and Archives Canada/PA-037596.

HBC tripmen hauling out a York boat at the beginning of Robinson Portage in 1878.

to the next landing stage. Although his view of the future was not entirely fulfilled in that the road he envisioned was never built, it turned out that he was close because we soon discovered that a basic transportation track had been installed.

As I suspected, the trolley did not measure up to Ken's expectations. As soon as the York was dragged up the rollers onto it, the wheels sunk in the soft earth. I had made the same mistake some years before in building a wheeled platform to move my own boat. My wheels, as with Ken's, were much too small to handle the weight of the boat. The trolley idea, sensible though it may have seemed in distant Norway House, was abandoned. The only way to get the York up the first hill was with log rollers, sheer physical effort, and a lot of sweat. The same methods we would have to employ to take her all the way to the other end of the trail. While some of the crew prepared logs, Gordon and Wayne began to clear the brush to give us a workable trail. It wasn't long before the vicious rasp of two chainsaws echoed through the previously peaceful woods.

The chainsaws and axes reminded me that I like to cut firewood. It's a mindless sort of job designed to allow me time to think without interruption, or to leave my mind blank as I choose. I picked up an axe and helped clear the trail, allowing the nomadic part of my brain to go where it willed. Sometimes, because I constantly take on more projects than I can comfortably handle, I feel as though my thoughts are scattered all over my life. I have to make a conscious effort to gather them from wherever they settle. Out there at the beginning of Robinson Portage, with only hard physical labour to concern me, I let them fly where they wished, haphazard, but comfortable in their confusion.

Close to where I worked, Charlie, with David Chubb, sorted the baggage into individual loads. I stopped work for a moment and watched in amazement as John loaded about a hundred kilograms onto Charlie's back and made it fast to his tumpline. With the strap passed around his forehead and the lines across his shoulders and down his back, Charlie supported the heavy load without apparent effort. Then John encumbered David in the same fashion, with an almost identical weight.

I knew the tripmen of old would never have considered carrying a load less than 160–170 pounds (73–77 kilograms). I didn't expect to see today's temporary tripmen attempt to tackle the same feat. But some of them did their best. Twenty years before, I had trekked with Sherpas in the Nepalese Himalaya; they too, like the Cree, could carry enormous burdens over long distances.

Without a word, Charlie and David set off up the incline to walk all the way to the far-off unloading site. Once I had my part of the early trail cleared, I loaded up a lighter version of a tripman's load on my back, though without a tumpline. I preferred to make do with a load slung across my shoulders and back. Weighed down by an estimated twenty-five to thirty kilograms of baggage, I followed the two stalwart young Cree. Not once did they stop on the rugged hike, a journey of close to two kilometres. Long before I reached the trail's end they were jogging back for another load. My return trip was rather slower as I stopped repeatedly to photograph

Hudson's Bay Company voyageurs (tripmen) with their loads at a portage on the Hayes River route from Lake Winnipeg to York Factory.

various aspects of the route. Halfway back I met Ryan carrying, if possible, even more than either Charlie or David.

When this portage trail was in regular use in the last century, the tripmen carried loads the equivalent of those our crew would bear on this expedition. Those hardy outdoors men trotted most of the way from one side to the other, not because they wanted the exercise, rather to get the loads off their backs as soon as possible. In fact, even novice tripmen ran Robinson Portage in both directions, without stopping for longer than it took to take on a load at one end or to drop a load at the other. Anyone who could carry a total of 1,200 pounds (2,640 kilograms) from one side to the other without a break was entitled to call himself a first-class tripman.[3]

Moving the York boats was, perhaps, easier for them than for us. At one time a form of railway line ran the length of the portage. Flat iron tracks were nailed to round wooden railroad ties hacked from the forest. Axles and wheels, which once supported railway carriages in a far-off land, made the long voyage by sea and river to be of use in this wilderness. We believe the individual tracks were attached to each other and kept the required distance apart by being nailed to slender tree trunks laid on the ground at right angles to the rails. The natural bearers then doubled as a cradle for the York boats. One assumes notches were cut in the ties to allow the railway wheel flanges to run smoothly on the flattened rails. With the York on rails and the tripmen pulling with their handlines, the portage might even have been a pleasant change from rapids and other portage routes. Running on rails, the York boats might not have needed unloading for the land crossing. Then again, those hills could have been a problem. For us there was no such historical luxury. Our York would have to be manhandled like the earliest boats on the Hayes River system.

Rusting in the undergrowth, a few of the axles and wheels remain to this day.[4] Lengths of flat iron, a few metres long, ripped off the ties and tossed into the woods, curl around trees and bushes like benign flattened serpents. Many of the wooden ties are still in their original positions on the trail. Crumbling with age and almost buried under the accumulated growth of decades, they are too old and too tired to bear any substantial weight. In order not to disturb their rest we stepped over them, not on them.

We looked longingly at the discarded rails and rolling stock. I found two rusted axles complete with wheels in otherwise good condition, though they proved to be of little use to us. There weren't enough decent straight lengths of iron to use as rails. The longest piece we found was probably no longer than the hull of the York. It was quicker and more efficient to make our own railway from nature's gifts: the forest fire's remains.

Had I known what the future held for us I would have stowed a length or two of flat iron on the York. It would definitely have come in useful. With the advantage of hindsight, one of those sections of flat rail could have been attached to the bottom of the keel. A strong iron shoe running the length of the keel would have protected it from damage and saved us many hours of work.

Ken McKay felt we could get the boat across the portage by late the following day. It was hard to agree or disagree as when he said it she was only half a length from the river she had recently left. The general consensus was that the York would reach the other side once she had crossed all the many obstacles in her path: whether it took one day, or two, or three, only time would tell. In anticipation of a quick traverse, Ken opted to make camp at the far end of the portage.

Psychologically it was a reasonably inspired idea; we would have the camp as an additional goal to strive for. Physically, the idea created yet another challenge. At the close of each day's work, tired and hungry, we were in for long walks to get our meals and to reach our tents.

I would have positioned the camp at the halfway point, then moved it to the far end when the boat reached that spot, but I wasn't in charge. As it turned out, Ken's plan worked well enough. Walking through the woods, with no heavy burdens, by day or by night, was a pleasant experience for us all. We had the chance to digest our cholesterol-laden meals returning to work. And we had the chance to slow down gradually after our labours, rather than collapsing straight into bed.

Ken O. and Ben loaded themselves with camp kitchen supplies. Adequately burdened, they made their way up the hill and out of sight. Being a resourceful man, Ken O. left enough food and cooking equipment at a point where he felt we might possibly get the boat to that night. He was out by a couple of hundred metres but no one really cared when it came to dinnertime.

The sound of an outboard motor strayed through the noises of a construction crew hard at work. Soon a lone canoe spluttered into view with two men aboard. Ranging far afield from Norway House, they were on a hunting trip. Hearing the chainsaws from out on Robinson Lake, they guessed it was the York boat expedition and had come to help. They were a welcome addition to the force, even for a single night.

Gordon unstepped the mast, everyone took hold of the lines and, at 6:30 p.m., the York began her slow tortuous passage overland from one stretch of whitewater to another, calmer, stretch of river. Shadows were lengthening, casting discreetly moving silhouettes of shrubs and trees across the trail. The air grew still. The only sounds were the dull roar of the waterfall and the laboured grunts of human intrusion.

A voice grumbled about having to work so hard on a Saturday night as the York stubbornly resisted our attempts to move her.

"I could have gone to a dance back at Norway House."

Everyone laughed and stopped for a second to wipe the sweat from dirty faces.

"One, two, three. HEAVE!" Wayne shouted.

We dug our heels in, leaned into our ropes and forced ourselves to take a step forward and upward. The York trembled, lurched slightly and turned the rollers hesitantly.

"And again. HEAVE!"

Wayne's desperate cry spurred us on. The boat moved a little more. Two rollers had passed under the stern. I grabbed them and ran forward to place them ahead of the dozen or so still in front of us. It was dangerous work. Late in the evening, working in the dark with the York moving well for a change, a long roller was kicked aside by the boat's passing and trapped the sole of my boot. I managed to throw myself sideways into the bushes to avoid a potentially serious injury. Others also came close to being trapped or hit by heavy logs swinging out of control that night. Tripmen of a century and more ago were equally at risk when moving heavy York boats over log rollers.

By mid evening we were halfway up the first slope, having covered less than a hundred metres. The cooks called us to dinner and we were delighted to have such a short distance to go for our meal. Leaning back against trees, with our bellies full and mugs of steaming coffee in our grimy hands, we talked of a name for the York.

"Based on the average comments so far today, I think we should call her, *Come on you son of a bitch, MOVE*," was my offering: a suggestion which was received with guffaws of laughter.

It's true we don't have a name for her, though many ideas have been put forward. In a more serious moment, I ventured that *Cree Pride* might be a worthwhile contender for the title. Much later, after we'd finished with Robinson Portage, I thought perhaps she should have been named *Ahkumenihtamowin*, the Cree syllabic word for perseverance. As it happened, no decisions were made for her baptism that evening. In fact, she never did receive a formal name, usually being referred to as *that York boat* by the crew and *Yorkie* by me.

Wayne rolled himself a cigarette, lit it, and got to his feet.

"Let's go, boys," he said, pulling on a pair of torn working gloves.

As that long night wore on, working in darkness for much of the time, we pushed over dead trees by brute strength, we cut down others with chainsaws, and, with felling axes, we trimmed logs and positioned them one in front of the other a few paces apart. We swatted mosquitoes and flies, we pushed and pulled the boat, we swore, we sweated, and by dint of sheer effort we made our heavy York boat defy gravity and roll up that long bitch of a hill. At 1:30 a.m., exhausted and with so far still to go, we called it a night. This time we had reached our initial goal. The York was sitting on rollers on top of the first hill.

The muscle-burning work was over for that day, but we weren't finished yet. We then had to walk, perhaps stagger would be closer to the truth for some of us, to the other end of the trail and put up our tents before we could sleep. At least one of the crew slept in the open, preferring to risk the mosquito attacks than waste valuable sleeping time erecting a tent in the dark. At 2:30 a.m. Robinson Portage fell silent, apart from the chorus of snores emanating from the campsite at one end.

A slow start was the inevitable introduction to Sunday morning. We, some of us, washed in the clear cold waters of the Hayes River at the foot of the rapids. It was refreshing and an excellent start to our day.

Back at camp, breakfast was soon ready. Our cooks had made a stack of fried eggs and bacon, with freshly baked bannock to soak up the grease. Urns of black tea and black coffee bubbled beside the wood fires. I actually felt fit that morning and ready for a tough day. Our two unexpected helpers of the previous evening had vanished. They were back on their hunting trip. We were thankful for their brief presence and the extra pairs of hands.

As we were about to leave, a party of Americans, on their way out after a wilderness fishing trip to Max Lake, arrived in two aluminium skiffs. State troopers from Minnesota, they were on their way home via the Hayes River to Molson Lake, where a float plane was to pick them up. We were on our way back along the trail so we helped them drag their boats and saved them an arduous hour in the process.

As we walked we explained what we were doing in the woods. None of those Americans had any idea what a York boat looked like. They stopped and stared in astonishment when they caught sight of old *Yorkie* sitting bolt upright in the middle of a forest. Our verbal descriptions of the boat we were portaging had obviously not been adequate to convey the true situation.

We were immediately bombarded with questions. One trooper wanted to know how we managed to drag such a big and heavy boat up the hill. Another asked if we had rowed it along the Echimamish River, and wondered aloud how we had negotiated all the beaver dams. Charlie answered the questions with pride in his voice. In a few minutes he told them how a dedicated crew fought the York over the beaver dams. The same way the crew were tackling the current job: brute force mixed with a little science.

The young troopers stood in the middle of the York for a group photograph, convinced that no one at home would believe their story without proof. They kindly offered to help us for an hour in return for our assistance to them. We declined the offer, knowing we had little chance of getting her ready to move for some time. Having just come from the steep hill Charlie called Max Portage, the fishing party were quick to advise that the approach to the next portage would cause us grief.

"The bottom of the lake is all boulders, close to the surface. You'll never get that big boat in to shore."

They left us with their thanks, three loaves of thinly sliced white bread, a can of gasoline, and some worn work gloves; all of the items gratefully received by our crew. Charlie was given a tall straw hat, which rarely left his head after that morning.

We were right to decline the offer of help, because by mid morning the boat hadn't moved at all. That didn't mean we had been slacking. While one team laid down the next long section of track and positioned log rollers, others removed nuisance obstacles such as tree stumps and large rocks. Up ahead another team widened the trail, a time-consuming operation in itself.

While the trail was being prepared for the York's next run, a lot more of our gear had been carried from one end of the track to the other. Every time anyone went ahead, for any reason, they carried something with them. No one wasted a trip, especially if they had to go to the camp. Walking back empty-handed was a treat, though we still tended to cover the ground at a trot. Gradually the mound of equipment on one side was transferred to the other.

More and more, during the trials and tribulations of Robinson Portage, I began to feel part of the team. Ken McKay and Ken Ormand, plus Charlie, Gordon, and Wayne, had always included me in conversation, other than decision-making discussions held in Cree. As we progressed over the portage the remaining crew members slowly accepted my presence. My fitness level was high and my ribs felt fine. All in all I was content to be in the Manitoba wilderness and quite happy with the expedition. I was enjoying myself as much as the Cree were.

We placed the next section of track right on top of the now useless railroad ties from the past. On one long, straight, downward slope the trail had to be built up with thick logs and earth on one side to keep the track level. While one group cut the undergrowth to widen the trail, another made use of any movable piece of wood or stone which would help level it. The difference in height from one side to the other was as much as a metre in places.

That section could have been really tough, especially if the boat had slid off the rails on the wrong side. In places where the drop on one side was a metre or more, after the track had been levelled, we had to be especially alert. An accident there would have been detrimental to the York's well-being and ours. Aware of the risk, we all hung on to the opposite side, away from the drop, ensuring that if, or when, the boat came off the rails, it had level ground to fall on and we would not be under it.

We cut long, slender tree trunks, blackened by fire, and stripped them of their dead branches. Two at a time we carried them on sore shoulders to the required position. Sometimes, when we had a straight run for a while, we were able to employ as many as ten trees, each six or seven metres long, end to end for each side of the track. Once roughly positioned, the thinner ones were pegged to keep them the required distance apart. The thicker ones, being proportionately heavier, didn't need to be held.

Slowly, the wooden railway crawled over the land. At times it ran on top of the old track, at other times it stretched beside it. Much of our route was dictated by the density of the bush, grown up since the last forest fire, and the state of the terrain. As closely as we could we followed the original path used by those who had fought their way over this land so long ago.

When the boat moved, we had up to eighty metres of track to run on. Rarely did we manage to cover more than a third of that distance before we lost control; often far less. Each brutal pull on the lines moved the boat a few more metres. Each hard-won metre took us closer to our ultimate destination. Every time the boat rolled smoothly it sounded like distant thunder roaring through the forest.

Wayne took on the role of cheerleader most of the time, constantly exhorting us to greater effort. Charlie added his voice, roaring back at Wayne and at the crew. Always, from both men, the cries were complimentary, especially from Charlie to Wayne as the latter had a natural ability to see problems and think his way out. Charlie alternated between calling him "Wayne the Pain" and "Wayne the Brain."

When the going was especially hard I found myself grunting the harsh guttural lyrics of the song of the Volga River boatmen. They seemed ideal for the situation:

A-ay ukhnyem! A-ay ukhnyem!
Yeshshto razik, yeshtsho da ras!
Yo-o heave ho! Yo-o heave ho!
Once again, one more time![5]

On a slight downhill incline, the York moved and gradually gathered momentum, gravity becoming our ally for a change. With shouts of joy, everyone worked to keep her moving and on the rails. Twenty-five metres slid under her keel before she twisted to one side and plunged into the bush. Undaunted, we collected the track from behind and re-positioned it in front. Scratched by bushes and treated mercilessly by insects, we manhandled the York out of the undergrowth and back on track.

And so it went on. Move a few metres, struggle for many minutes. Move a little more and crash off the rails. Lift, grunt, push, groan, pull, moan, stop, swear. Pleasure became synonymous with a wooden boat rumbling across rough country on uneven log wheels. When Wayne ran out of vocal steam Charlie could always be relied on to take over.

"Come on, boys. You're the best!" he bellowed and the crew responded immediately.

Throughout the long day the forest echoed with the grunts and groans of us all. Mingled with the expressions of effort and pain, the chainsaws ripped noisily into wood, while long-handled felling axes rang musically each time they bit into a tree or a log. No matter how hard the work, how tired their bodies might be, everyone kept their sense of humour. Rarely did an hour go by when the laughter of the irrepressible Cree wasn't heard.

Occasionally we got a good run and the boat stayed on track for a change. Then we all became excited and even noisier. That's when we seemed to have more energy; our hearts lifted, broad smiles covered tired faces. We felt we could move mountains. When the York was stuck hard, when, deep inside, we felt it could never move again, from somewhere we drew on unknown reserves of strength. Each time we managed the impossible.

The mosquitoes, blackflies, and other aerial demons made our lives absolutely miserable. There was no way to kill them all so we finally gave up trying. Murray and I, as always, were their main targets. We tried to ignore them and suffered the misery in silence. We knew that, eventually, we would get back on the river and leave them behind. We just didn't know when.

Each bush, each shrub, each leaf, each blade of grass had its dependant clouds of fierce winged devils, watching and waiting for living containers of red blood to pass by. They attacked en masse. They stung, we slapped. They bit, we itched. Hopelessly outnumbered, though we slaughtered them in their thousands, we had little chance: they inevitably won the battles.

Murray and I passed bug spray back and forth and moaned at the torment as the work progressed and the itching got worse. Unlike the celebrated Lieutenant John Franklin, who would never kill any creature, we had murder in our hearts. Franklin was content to blow on the dreaded insects to remove them. He was reported to have explained, "The world is wide enough for us both."[6] On Robinson Portage we found it impossible to agree with his gentle philosophy.

We dragged the York up hills. We dragged her down hills. We forced her through the bush. We lifted her over immovable rocks. We dragged her past living trees. Thinking of the great pyramids of Egypt, and the vast human resources the Pharoahs were able to muster to transport massive blocks of stone from the far-off quarries to Gizeh, made me long for a few more men. At one obstacle I gasped out the need for a few slaves to help us.

"We are slaves. We just need more Indians," Wayne answered. "There's too many chiefs around here."

Instant humour and subsequent laughter were guaranteed to spur us on.

"As far as I can see there are too many Indians, anyway," I countered with what little breath I had. More laughter and a little harmless sniping at me followed.

The hours passed. Morning changed into afternoon. Afternoon turned into night. Aching muscles tightened and cramped, lungs felt like they were ready to burst. Eyes became red-rimmed from salty sweat. Hands, faces, and bodies were grimed with the brown of the soil, the green of living bushes, and the black of long-dead trees.

A-ay ukhnyem! A-ay ukhnyem!

Many of us endured cuts and scrapes, adding congealed rivulets of bright red blood to the exotic patterns bestowed on us by the forest. By dark we looked like a Native raiding party camouflaged with war paint.

One hill, which we coasted down with relative ease as the light began to fail, ended in soft, swampy ground. A miniature creek ran across our path, weakening the already springy earth. The bushes on both sides hemmed in the trail and, being on wet land, harboured the expected airborne squadrons of ravenous tormentors. That hollow gave us much grief.

We cut down the bushes and used them as mats to reinforce the footing. We massacred mosquitoes, taking no captives. The mosquitoes ripped into us in retaliation, determined to drain our veins. Our log rollers subsided into the mud. We sunk into the mud. To add to our woes, as we attempted to drag the York over the morass, we had to make a turn to the right. Not a sharp turn, but a turn which, given the York's length, caused us unwarranted trouble.

No one shirked. Anxious to get out of that hole we found reserves of strength we hadn't imagined. The York, stubborn as usual, was reluctant to move. Our combined strength was not enough to persuade her to roll. All our efforts proved fruitless; something else was holding us back. Wayne got down flat on the ground, his face in the mud, to study the problem.

"Look at this, Ken," he called.

Ken crouched beside him and muttered something incomprehensible. I took a look as well. A flat metal bar, which had been screwed down the length of the sternpost, bent underneath and screwed into the keel as a protective shoe, had been torn from its position. Instead of being protection and added strength for the join at keel and stern, it had curled into a tight circle. Each time the steel coil came up against a log it acted as a perfect brake. Charlie removed the remaining screws and formally presented the badly bent bar to Ken. There was nothing to stop us after that.

Wayne shouted and we pushed and pulled. Using their tumplines round their shoulders, four of the biggest guys harnessed themselves like draught horses to the bow. Led by Charlie, they leaned into their makeshift bridles and strained, their heels dug into the earth. We put our shoulders to the sides and the stern.

A-ay ukhnyem! A-ay ukhnyem!

She moved a little. We paused for breath, gathering our strength. We tried again. The York began to move. Once we got it on dry land again and with a straight uphill run ahead, we sagged. At 9:40 p.m., with about five hundred metres still to go, we gave up the struggle for the second night and crawled back to our sleeping bags.

Ken Ormand, our unofficial chaplain, wrote a prayer to help us over that long portage. He asked me to rewrite it in correct English for him. I read it, made one small change, and handed it back. By virtue of its simplicity and humility it was already close to perfection. He didn't need my help. With his permission I share it with all who, by reading this book, share something of the hardships of those two days of long hours on Robinson Portage.

> Oh Great Spirit
> Thou art Mighty and Holy.
> Give us and renew our strength
> to be ready each day
> as we travel across your waters
> and through your rough
> beautiful land.
> Guide us Great Spirit
> not to grow weary.
> We will walk and we will row
> and not be weak.
> Great Spirit,
> We give into your hands, to look after,
> our wives, children and other loved ones
> we left behind.
> Thank you.

We have trust in you
that you will answer our prayers.
In Jesus's name. Amen.

Monday morning dawned much too soon for most of us. I hauled my aching bones out of my sleeping bag, unzipped the tent, and stood up in the fresh air of a northern dawn. The riverbank was down a steep slope to my left. I staggered down to wash in the ice-cold water. Others had already been there and someone had left a wet bar of soap on a flat rock and a soaking-wet towel on a tree.

I stripped to the waist and crouched barefoot on the cold granite. Thus exposed I became a target of anything with wings and a cruel bite. As usual, the Manitoban wilderness squadrons were in no mood to show mercy to anyone. They were airborne and they were hungry.

Splashing myself with cold water, I washed my upper body as quickly as possible. The top half washed and fairly clean, I protected it with my shirt and removed the lower half of my clothing. There was no false modesty in keeping parts of my body covered, nothing more than a desire to avoid getting bitten.

Under other circumstances I, and the others, would have jumped into the water and had a swim and a wash at the same time. The multitude of long fat leeches,[7] wriggling over the rocks and weeds in the river, convinced us to stay on dry land and suffer the flying midgets from hell. I wondered how Franklin had fared with the leeches nearly two centuries before. When he fell in, not far from where I washed, leeches must have been present. Did he feel there was room enough for them also?

That morning, before breakfast, John Wesley went back along the trail to pick up a sack of flour dropped near the halfway mark the day before. He found a bear had beaten him to it and ripped it open, scattering flour in all directions. Fortunately, it had left enough for us so that Simon Clynes, our baking expert, could make up a stack of bannock for breakfast and lunch. At least John was spared the effort of carrying a full bag.

After breakfast, Ken McKay stood up and started back along the trail, now well flattened by our constant movements. Charlie called out to remind him of the morning prayer; voicing what others were thinking. That was the first morning our captain had forgotten the spiritual well-being of his crew. Like the rest of us, he was tired. Ken O. recited his prayer for Robinson Portage and we went back to work. I wouldn't have been at all surprised to see a black bear with a flour-white muzzle and paws watching us from the shadows. Perhaps it did, without our knowledge.

Dinner on Sunday night had been white beans and salt pork. By the time we reached the York the beans were showing their effect on a few of the guys — yet another raucous sound to pervade the wilderness, adding a rich aromatic human tone to nature's exotic fragrances. Perhaps that's why we never did see that bear.

That morning a float plane flew low over Robinson Portage. We could see it through the trees, but it was unlikely that they could see us or the boat. They may, however, have spotted our tents in the clearing by the river.

When we first hauled the York out of the water, two days before, I had suggested to Ken that we take advantage of the situation and re-caulk the hull. He said we would do it once the boat was on the far side of the portage, which made sense as the boat was sure to suffer from the rigours of the land crossing. As it happened, the York took a terrible pounding at Robinson. Every time it came off the rollers it groaned as if in pain. Few other wooden boats of that size and weight would have survived the journey. It is to Ken McKay's credit as a boat-builder that our York was still in one piece after two gruelling days.

At midday we had reached the campsite. Only a short, steep, muddy hill and a few metres of swamp separated the York from the Hayes River. We broke camp and moved all personal gear, tents, and assorted equipment to the dry rocks, ready for reloading.

Four of the team went back to the starting point to collect the canoe, all the oars, the mast, and a few other bits and pieces. The oars and mast could have been tied tightly together and tracked down the rapids with a rope, saving the trouble of carrying them. Instead, they were manhandled with the canoe. At least the trolley Ken had fabricated to carry the York now became useful. Two of the guys tied the canoe, oars, mast, and whatever else was left to the trolley and pulled it overland. It ran much faster and infinitely more smoothly than the York.

While the final load was on its way, the rest of us built a log ramp well into the river to clear the thick mud and tall reeds on the shoreline. The mosquitoes came to see what was going on, had many a meal and did nothing to help.

By 1:00 p.m. all the equipment, the boat, the canoe, and all the men were finally on the same side of the portage. Gradually *Yorkie* was lowered down the mud slope until her bow was on the first log of the ramp. There she stuck fast. We tried rollers under her keel, all

Large freight canoes and their crews at the end of a portage. Getting back on the river after the exertions of the portages was always a relief for the men.

the way along. We pushed, we pulled, we lifted. We exerted all our strength. She would not move. The problem was that the rollers were sinking in the soft ground and ceased to turn. The friction between keel and logs was too great to allow movement.

At that moment I conjured up a memory from a photographic assignment in Norway two years before. There, at Mellemvaerftet,[8] a traditional boat-building yard on the west coast, wooden boats were hauled out of the water on a tilted framework of timber, like a cradle. The cradle, in nautical parlance — the ways, had been greased to ease the passage of the boats, up and down the slope. I suggested we take one of the tubs of lard and spread its contents thickly on the middle of the logs and wherever could be reached on the keel.

Wayne said he had already suggested that, but no one took any notice. They did when I explained it was once accepted practice to launch a boat on greased rails. While Wayne smeared the thick, white, pork fat on the keel and on the log ramp, I grabbed one of my cameras. Trying to keep my feet from getting wet, I leapt from dry tussock to dry tussock, through the swampy foreshore, to the rocks to record the final few metres. I had expected to hear the call to halt just out of reach of the water. The boat's position would have been perfect for re-caulking the seams. I didn't hear the call. No one gave the order.

With help from the pork fat, the York slid smoothly onto the ramp, rolled down the incline a few metres, and was trundled straight off the end into the river. Murray climbed aboard and poled her over to the rocks where I stood by the mound of baggage. Ken and crew followed my trail to the rocks. I asked Ken about the caulking. He said we would do it later because he wanted to keep moving. There was little point in arguing so we cleaned out the residue of leaves and twigs that had collected over the previous two days, laid out the blue tarpaulin in the bottom, and started loading. By the time the baggage had been sealed against the elements by wrapping it in the tarpaulin, water was already trickling in through a few seams.

At 6:00 p.m., fifty-two-and-a-half hours after we had first arrived at the top of the falls, we pushed off from the rocks at the bottom. Robinson Portage, our biggest challenge to date, had been overcome. No one had suffered more than superficial injury. We were fitter, more experienced, and ready for the next challenge. It felt good to be back on the river with all members of the expedition safely on board. The only disturbing note was that we were leaking like a sieve.

CHAPTER 10
Logan Lake and Whitewater

BACK ON THE RIVER, BAILING became a priority, which meant that I, as the spare hand, had to get busy with a plastic scoop, a thick sponge, and a large, white bucket. I scooped up the water and poured it into the bucket. When the bucket was full it weighed about twenty-five kilograms. I lifted it up from the bilges, tipped it over the side, and poured it out. I did that for a couple of hours. The long-dormant muscles I had revived on Robinson Portage were given more exercise. Crouched low in the bottom of the boat, my nose was altogether too close to the bilge. The fetid odour of swamp water clung to the lower inside of the hull. Bailing was not a lot of fun, but, I reasoned to myself, it was better than sinking.

Three kilometres of reed-choked river took us to the beginning of Logan Lake. There are two possible routes from this junction. One, the northern route, follows the Hayes River. The southern route covers the full length of Logan Lake, with a portage at the end. Both routes were used by canoes and certainly one by York boats. We, however, did not know which had been the preferred route.

The lake and portage looked shorter, while the Hayes River had a number of rapids to navigate. Ken chose the lake and the portage.

I wasn't sure which I would have chosen, although I did look longingly at the entrance to the Hayes as we passed. Ben told me it was not a good route. He said he had been there before and there was a very bad rapid on the Hayes. As darkness began to fall we made camp on a large, grassy ledge on the north shore of the lake. It was a heavenly spot. Behind us, and on either side, a barrier of spruce trees served as a windbreak. In front we had the smooth expanse of the lake.

The younger crew members went for a swim in the dark, while others relaxed with fishing rods. With the York unloaded I became aware that one of the kitchen chairs had not survived Robinson Portage. I was sure it was back there on the edge of the trail somewhere: another relic to rust in the woods, this one of more modern York boat days. I knew I would not miss it for a moment.

Over a dinner of cold macaroni, I talked with Ken about the many leaks in the hull. He said we would haul the boat out at Oxford House and effect repairs there. I was not convinced the boat would get that far in its battered condition, and said so, especially as it was about to suffer further indignities. My entreaties fell on deaf ears. The boat would be repaired at Oxford House.

Storm clouds were gathering as we went to bed. There was no rain that night, just a phenomenal display of lightning and the thunderous drumming of Thor's hammer.[1] At 5:00 a.m. the spectacle was repeated: a more than effective wake-up call for all the crew. That morning was the most beautiful we had experienced thus far. Sunbeams splayed all over the sky, like the fingers of God, from behind the clouds. Golden shafts of light illuminated the lake, creating irregular circles on the surface, like distorted spotlights in a theatre.

While Ken Ormand brewed up a big pot of coffee, I went for a swim in the cold, clear water by myself, revelling in the freshness and the solitude and enjoying a different form of exercise. As I scrambled back up the rocks to my clothes, I carefully checked my body and limbs for leeches. There were none.

Drinking scalding coffee, munching on leftover bannock, and loading the boat that morning was a leisurely affair, consequently, we didn't leave until after 8:00 a.m.: we were all still too tired after the heavy exercise of Robinson Portage. Once on the water, however, the rowers' adrenaline began to flow again as they responded to Ken's exhortations. An hour later we arrived close to the head of the lake.

That landing was, if possible, an improvement even on the previous night's campsite. A natural clearing sloped to the water with a surround of firs marching slowly up the hill. Lichen spread over the larger rocks like fine-coloured lace. The flatter ledges were hidden, for the most part, under a soft, springy carpet of caribou moss. A grouping of bare level rocks shaded by an old spruce by the water's edge made a perfect kitchen site. Wild cranberries littered the open glades between the trees. Not having had breakfast, other than the coffee and a bite of bannock, we were hungry. We filled our mouths with the juicy, slightly bitter red berries while the cooks prepared something a little less healthy to placate our complaining stomachs.

Charlie and three others went in the canoe to check out the portage access and route. No one was looking forward to the job. After the strain of Robinson Portage, we all knew it would not be easy. The Americans had told us the lake bottom leading to the portage was a mess of large, round boulders. They were guaranteed to cause us trouble.

Not far away was Max Lake, our route to the next part of the Hayes River. Unfortunately, it was on the other side of a remarkably high, well-forested hill: a daunting prospect in itself. Charlie repeatedly referred to the hill as Max Portage. In the old days it was known, with some justification, as Hill Portage.

Overhead, two bald eagles performed an aerial ballet for our entertainment. On the ground there were many tracks of small animals and some bear scat farther up the hill. As usual, with a relatively large group of people, there was so much loud chatter that apart from the eagles, we saw no other wildlife. By this time each member of the crew, except myself and the two Kens, wore eagle feathers in their hair or tucked into their hats. Although I found a number of elegant-looking feathers, I decided it would be presumptuous of me to copy the other guys and wear one in my hat.

To help pass the time until Charlie came back, I went for a walk in the woods to photograph wildflowers. Some distance inland I came upon distinct moose tracks and followed them for a while. They made a large semicircle around the head of the lake and often intersected other trails. The more distance I placed between me and the riverbank where the crew rested, the quieter it became. Even though I couldn't see them, I could hear small creatures rustling through the undergrowth.

I was intrigued by the variety and colours of the lichen. Arctic explorers, on the verge of starvation, used to boil lichen, which they called *tripe de roche*, and eat it.[2] I wondered if the lichen around me was the same rock tripe. My interest in its flavour, however, was not strong enough to taste it, nor was my hunger sharp enough.

When I returned, Ken Ormand expressed concern that I had been gone so long. There are many advantages to an adult life of leading wilderness expeditions; trekking in the forests of western Canada, the jungles of west and central Africa, and the mangrove forests of Bangladesh. I explained to Ken that, if I could safely and successfully track a tiger through dense jungle bush on foot,[3] and find my way back to base, the Manitoba backwoods were unlikely to pose a problem for me.

The recce (reconnaissance) crew came back at 10:15 a.m. with demoralizing news. Their estimate was two days to get to Max Lake. The imminent portage involved dragging the York over the ten metres of submerged boulders through the shallows, as we had been warned. Beyond that chore, the route was a mere five hundred metres, up and over an unpleasantly steep hill through a stand of large trees.

Listening to Charlie explaining the difficulties, I wondered how long it would be before we actually got started on the job. Ken and Gordon McKay decided to take a look at the problems themselves. We stretched out in the sun again to wait. An hour later they returned and described what they had seen. Their description, not surprisingly, matched the report Charlie had already given. Ken asked me if I thought the old York boat crews had used the portage. I told him that, according to my research, both routes were used. I added that the Franklin expedition, coming upriver, had tackled the northern route through the rapids known variously as Hell Gates or Hill Gates; Ben's bad rapid, I assumed. I felt sure the majority of York boat crews would have kept to the river whenever possible and I said so.

Months later, after reading many more articles and books about the fur-trade era, and the Hayes River route in particular, I partially changed my mind. Now I feel that, knowing the terrain and looking for the easiest possible route, the tripmen would have used the rapids to go downriver and, with the smaller boats, the portage to return. Hill Portage would not be a difficult prospect coming upstream from Max Lake to Logan Lake. The steep hill is on the Logan side. The incline from the crest to Max Lake is gentle in comparison. Downhill travel is an exercise in gravity, requiring far less effort. Writing of his 1819 journey on the Hayes River, Lieutenant John Franklin commented on the use of both routes: "… We… arrived at a shallow reedy lake [Max Lake], the direct course through which leads to the Hill Portage. This route has, however, of late years been disused, and we therefore turned towards the north, and crossing a small arm of the lake [Opiminigoka] arrived at Hill Gates by sunset."[4]

Ken McKay decided to take a look at the rapids on the alternate northern route leading to Hell Gates with Charlie and Gordon. The three of them cruised away in the canoe, leaving at 11:30 a.m. With a round trip of about forty kilometres to cover, they were unlikely to be back for three hours at least. Some of the crew settled back on the tarpaulin, spread across the mossy clearing, and closed their eyes. I found a comfortable seat on the rocks with a natural granite backrest and wrote my journal. Above us, rain clouds gathered, the sun breaking through occasionally. There was enough of a warm breeze to keep the bugs away. Under different circumstances the day would have been exceedingly enjoyable. The location and the view reminded me of my own home in the Gulf Islands of British Columbia. For a self-sufficient backwoods person, or persons, it would have been a near-perfect site on which to build a home.

Wayne and Ryan fished awhile. They had a net on board, so they took one end out into the middle of the lake with the York and secured it to a buoy. The other end was tied to a tree stump on the shore. Floats kept the net visible and in place. I watched with interest. A fish dinner or two was a distinct possibility. With that flurry of activity over, the guys settled back again and waited. Ken O. talked of going to look at the steep portage.

I offered to go with him, getting up and stretching. Ryan stood up, as well. The three of us worked our way through the tangled undergrowth on the vegetation-draped cliff overlooking the lake. After some distance we crossed a beaver trail running from the water's edge, up a steep muddy incline, to a few symmetrically chewed tree stumps.

"Beavers don't often come that far from water," Ryan told me in surprise.

The boulder-strewn approach to the portage was clearly visible through the water from our elevated position. We all agreed it would be a wet and thoroughly miserable task to get the boat out of the water there. The underwater hazards would greatly increase the possibility of seriously damaging the York and ourselves.

The hill, as Charlie had said, was steep: about forty-five degrees for most of its length. Once on top the obvious trail wound its way down through the forest to an easy launching site at Max Lake. Because of the York boat's size, a few healthy trees bordering the trail would have to be cut down.

In truth, none of us liked the idea of trying to get her up the hill, or around the turns on the other side. There was no guarantee we would even be able to get the York up such a steep hill. Although, having seen what those healthy young Cree could achieve, I'm sure the heavy York boat would have reached the top eventually. If we tried, however, and she got away from us, those underwater rocks would make kindling out of her. The rapids began to look like a decidedly more practical option. On the way back, Ryan pointed out a new lynx trap under a tree, close to the path. Someone was obviously trapping in the area.

At the camp the net was being pulled in and a decent catch of pike and pickerel added to our larder. That night, wherever we happened to be, there had to be fish on the menu for dinner. However, the best and most mouth-watering plans can and do go wrong. We didn't have fish that night as I had hoped. We didn't have it the following night, either. We did, finally, get around to feasting on the lake's delicacies two days later for lunch.

Our only map, now getting torn and grubby, was spread out on the rocks as I tried to calculate the distances left from point to point via Hell Gates. Wayne and David came over to watch. They asked me which way I thought their forefathers had travelled. I repeated that I was sure they would have stuck to the river as much as possible. They nodded, perhaps in agreement, perhaps simply in understanding. Any time I opened our precious map, a few would gather round to find out where we were. On those occasions, I pointed out our approximate location and heads nodded wisely, including those who could not read a map. Our daily position, relative to Norway House, Oxford House, and, at times, to York Factory, interested everyone. At the end of each day Ken normally asked me how far I thought we had travelled. Others asked how far to go before Oxford House. We began to speculate on when we would reach the halfway point.

The rapids reconnaissance party purred into view by mid-afternoon. They had explored the first few sets of rapids, and, although the last one would be tough to handle, were confident we could manage it. Ben told me again there was another rapid, a really big one, later on. He was talking about Hell Gates: he just didn't know it by that name. Ben was, however, very concerned about it. As it transpired, Ken and his two canoe partners hadn't gone that far to look at it, so we had no recent knowledge of its power. As we later discovered, it would have been a long trip to Hell Gates and back for the reconnaissance party.

The Cree, at least the Cree I was with, liked to discuss all options in detail and vote on that basis. In that respect they were truly democratic. A modern-day *powwow* began. I could only guess at most of the discussion, held as it was in the Cree language. It was apparent that they asked Ben's advice, or sought his knowledge. I found that strange as many of them had openly laughed at his quiet, shy ways. He was, however, the only one among us who had actually seen each of the rapids on the next few kilometres of the Hayes River. Charlie had travelled all the way from Norway House to York Factory by canoe, in 1985 — nine years before. He had carried his lightweight craft over the hill to Max Lake, bypassing the potentially dangerous rapids on that section of the Hayes.

At 4:25 p.m. the decision was made. We would take the northern route down the rapids on the Hayes River. Ken had asked the crew to vote for the route of their choice. They had voted evenly, six for the portage, six for the rapids. Wayne pointed out, in Cree (followed by a quick translation to English for me), that there were thirteen of us, indicating me as he did so, therefore there could not be a tied vote.

I didn't understand most of the words of his statement in Cree, nor any of the replies. It wasn't important to understand the words. The meanings were clear. Although Wayne, and perhaps some of the others, thought my voice should be heard, as an outsider I did not rate a vote. In a way those who excluded me were right. It was their expedition, not mine. Ken McKay, as captain, made the final decision. It suited me well enough because that was how I would have voted, anyway.

With the best part of a day having been wasted, we then had to backtrack almost the full length of Logan Lake— against the wind. The crew rowed and sweated in the late-afternoon humidity. I crouched in the bilge, also sweating, bailing out water — bucket after tedious bucket — and tried to ignore its stagnant smell.

The first set of swifts was in front of us within minutes of turning off the lake onto the Hayes River. By then I was standing on a rowing bench by the mast, where I could see clearly. There was nothing serious to impede our progress, just a lot of miniature whirlpools, a glassy look on the surface and a series of mild riffles. The rowers kept their rhythm as the York increased its speed with the current. After a few more swifts, much worse was to come.

John Wesley was steering as we approached the next small rapid. His strength was not equal to our needs on that occasion. He got us hung up on a rock almost on top of the slight drop. Gordon vaulted over the other rowers to take his place while the rest of us fended off the rocks with our oars. As a team, we slipped through to calmer water.

The light was starting to fade as we ghosted up toward Oskatukaw Rapids, the last one Ken had looked at earlier that day. I thought he was leaving it far too late to give the order to back water. He, however, showed no concern as his eyes flicked from the whitewater to a rock wall on our left. In truth I fully anticipated a fast run down the 125 metres or so of rapids, a crash against the rocks, and a potential upset. Ken timed our approach to perfection.

Wayne stood on the foredeck with a mooring line in his hand. David and I stood behind him, similarly equipped. As we closed the last possible place to get ashore, a steeply sloping granite rock on the edge of the falls, Charlie yelled at Wayne in Cree. He didn't move. I shouted at him.

"Go now or we're all dead."

He went, scrambling up the almost sheer rock like a lizard. David followed, helped by a none-too-gentle push from me. I was right behind him. To my left, Edward jumped in unison with me, to land two metres away. The four of us held on to the lines with every muscle quivering.

At the stern, Charlie had hurled himself onto a ledge and made his line fast to a bush. We secured ours and the York came to a stop with her bow no more than two metres from the lip of the falls. Wayne looked at me and managed a smile.

"Did you hear what Charlie shouted at me?" he asked. I shook my head.

"He told me the same as you: 'Go now or we're dead.'" He laughed as he said it.

We had been lucky. Ken had placed us in the perfect position to get ashore, but the agility and the strong arms of his crew had saved the York. The potential for disaster had been right there. We should, perhaps, have gone ashore at the other side of the river, where the bank was so much lower, for safety. Holding the York would still have been a strain, but less hazardous to our health. Against that, however, was a series of rocks close to shore, lining the river bend. The most comfortable campsite was, of course, on the hill above us where a level clearing covered in springy moss awaited. The best and shortest portage route crossed the same hill. Ken's decision had been correct. It was just a little hard on our nerves.

From the high rocks in the twilight, the whitewater, curling over the boulders beneath us and gouging the opposite river bank, looked threatening. In the morning we would find out how bad it actually was.

Following another dinner of cold macaroni and stale bannock, a light rain sent us to bed at 10:00 p.m. We needed rest before the trials of the next day.

After the falls, at the base of the high campsite, a near-perfect landing stage presented itself. The portage was no more than twenty metres and downhill, no less. We loaded ourselves with as much baggage as each of us could carry on our backs; then picked up another item in each hand. Weighed down, we soon had everything, including the canoe, moved and ready for reloading.

The York was a different proposition. Although there is an obvious canoe route close to the high rock, it was too narrow for the big boat. Ken and the crew took the York back upriver a hundred metres or so, crossed to the lower bank and secured it. I watched from high on the cliff as Charlie gesticulated with his arms, telling each man where to stand and what to do. His instructions and positioning were spot-on. As they slowly but skillfully tracked the York down the rapids from one shore, I shot a roll of film from a high point on the other.

Around the next bend we encountered more rapids: the Ohoomisewe. Ken steered the boat into an obvious eddy on the left bank and waited while Charlie and I studied the route. There was an obvious chute close to the middle with enough clearance for the boat. We agreed that the Ohoomisewe posed no great problem for the York. We could run this next bit of turbulence without any problem. Taking a leaf out of the voyageurs guide book, Charlie

Library and Archives Canada/PA-169585.

A typical HBC scow racing down rapids. Wherever possible, tripmen ran the rapids rather than lose time on portages.

took the *gouvernail* position on the steering sweep, while I took on the role of *avant*,[5] kneeling in the bow. We told the crew to be ready to bring in their oars when ordered. Charlie called for some power and we moved out into the main stream. Using hand signals back to Charlie, I lined the stem and sternposts up with the central flow. The oars dug deep and we leaped forward. A few metres from the drop, Charlie yelled, "Oars up," and down we went in a flurry of oars waving in the air and a rush of racing river. The crew, riding backwards, whooped with excitement as we crashed through the spray to calmer waters.

While we challenged the whitewater, the canoe team stayed above the rapids, watching and waiting. Once we were safely down and drifting around in the corner of a large eddy, it was their turn. I could almost imagine Ken Ormand's standard admonishment to his passenger, "Sit still, Ben."

Charlie steered us closer to the right bank and rested the oars. I stood up, the better to see the canoe. They were a few minutes behind us and out of our vision for most of the time. Suddenly, the green prow raced around the bend, the canoe and two men leaning to the right. Ken O. straightened his craft and placed it squarely on course down the centre of the rapids. His position and style were classic. We cheered his success as he swung right to join us in the eddy, a broad smile over his happy face. Ben sat stony-faced, his white knuckles still clamped firmly on both sides of the canoe. To his credit he did crack a ghost of a smile when I winked at him.

According to a river runner's chart I studied later,[6] there are a series of pictographs, or rock drawings, along this section of the route, though we didn't see any.

Ducks were plentiful along that part of the Hayes River after the rapids. Encouraged by his pals, John Wesley stood up in the bow, loaded the shotgun, took aim at a low-flying duck, pulled the trigger and missed. I silently congratulated the duck on its good fortune. The crew jeered at John and urged him to try again. He did. He missed a second time and another duck flapped urgently past to safety. Perhaps the ducks had heard about the lack of respect accorded their two relatives and were playing hard to get.

For two hours, or thereabouts, we cruised grandly along the deep, placid river. The canoe kept station a little behind us and off to one side. In places, the river wasn't much wider than the extent of the oars. At times we passed through canyons of ancient rock rising steeply from the bottom of the river. Closed in by nature our trespassing voices echoed from side to side until they died away in whispers. The canyons gave way to forests and the forests to swamps. We spent much of that late afternoon cruising under the umbrellas of the white spruce and tamarack lining the river's boundaries. The rowers chattered among themselves in Cree as they forced the York onwards. I sat at the stern with Ken McKay for a long time, talking about the old days of the York boats on this fabulous river.

Turning left through a gradual bend, mindful of Ben's warning of a big rapid somewhere ahead, I returned to the bow to act as lookout. In the distance, perhaps two hundred metres beyond, a gleam of white caught my eye. I listened, but could hear nothing unusual over the booming of the oars. Hell Gates was in sight, if not yet audible.

"Whitewater ahead, Ken," I called, pointing to the distant surf. Ken nodded and signalled the rowers to slacken the pace. Charlie shipped his oar and came up to take a look.

"That's Ben's big rapid for sure," I said, more to myself than to Charlie. "I hope it doesn't live up to its name."

He nodded and pointed out a place to tie up the boat on the right bank. We would have to scout the route carefully. We could not afford a mishap at Hell Gates.

The Canoe Expedition,
Oxford House to York Factory

The broad expanse of Paktikonika Rapids. We spent an afternoon practising our skills on this magnificent stretch of whitewater.

Mark and Barb heading for the second set on Paktikonika.

Rob and Barb about to get very wet while running down the hill.

Rob looks for a way through a real rock garden while we wait patiently.

Rob and Val ferrying hard across the foaming current below the first set of Paktikonika Rapids.

Resting in an eddy after a long, wet ride down the hill.

A convenient group of rocks makes a good place to go ashore for lunch.

Rob cleaning pike for dinner — a regular event.

Mark and Rob handlining over a sharp rock ledge.

There is a good line through this mess of whitewater but it takes some scouting from the bank to find it.

Val and Barb handlining close in to the willow-covered riverbank.

Our campsite on the "Rock" beside the last big rapids on the Hayes River.

Two canoes and Rob's shotgun with Crane's Breast Cliff in the background at the confluence of the Hayes and Fox rivers. Note the York Factory logo on the gun's stock.

A quiet stretch of pebble beach beside the fast-flowing river.

York Factory. Our goal at the end of the Hayes River.

The author at York Factory after completing the Hayes River journey from Norway House.

CHAPTER 11
Near Disaster at Hell Gates

LEAVING KEN MCKAY, MURRAY, AND Wayne on board, the rest of us pushed our way through bushes and branches of trees to get a good look at the next hazard. The river was confined to a slot ten metres wide, running through a gorge of near-vertical granite. On our bank, where the side of the gorge was lowest, there were bushes and many trees right to the water's edge, plus soft, spongy ground cover and occasional limited access to the river.

Forming the opposite cliff, a large island of near-vertical rock towered over the flow, studded with a few trees. Behind it, a short portage led to a less exuberant part of the river, but too shallow for our boat. Neither side of the main stream appeared to offer particularly safe purchase for handlining. The consensus was that Hell Gates was a mean-looking bitch of a rapid, but we could handle it. I could only continue to hope it wouldn't live up to its sinister name. Franklin and his men had tracked their boat up this rapid in preference to battling their way over Hill Portage. To lighten the load, they portaged their cargo up the shallow route behind the rock island.[1] That route was not a viable option for our heavy boat.

An artist's rendition of a column of tripmen portaging boats and freight around a waterfall.

"We'll try it from this side." Charlie made a statement and, if his facial expression was anything to go by, posed a question to me at the same time. I agreed. Either side would have suited me. I didn't like one more than the other, but I had faith in Charlie's judgment and ability.

"We'll move it up to here." He indicated an indentation in the bank, like a small bay, where the water was relatively still. "We can unload here then handline it."

We went back and broke out the thickest mooring lines, four of them — each three centimetres thick, securing two each to bow and stern. Ken stayed at the steering oar, standing on the afterdeck. Charlie joined the remaining rowers on board, Murray and Wayne. All three held their oars ready to paddle, pole, or fend off as required. Carefully, we edged the big boat forward from the shore, getting her closer to the rim of the falls. The small trees and bushes at the river's side got in the way, forcing us to pass the lines over or around them to one another. John and I held one stern line. David and Edward manned the other. In front of us and out of our sight, Gordon and his team took care of the bow. Together we held the boat tight to the bank. We only needed to move her about four lengths to the unloading site.

The current, however, proved to be substantially stronger than we anticipated. We soon had to trot to keep up with the York. As the Hayes River swept her inexorably on toward the rapids, we crashed through bushes and slipped on slimy rocks. We were lucky none of us suffered ankle injuries. On board, Charlie and the guys did their best to apply the brakes, their oars digging deep against the flow. Between us we almost got her safely into the still area. Almost, but not quite.

The wind, which had been gusting playfully to push us along the river, turned against us. Still blowing from the same direction, it swept the stern away from the bank, putting additional strain on our eight arms. Almost beam on to the chosen unloading point, we lost her.

Ken, valiantly working to counteract the unexpected swing of the stern, turned his sweep marginally the wrong way and we were in trouble. The stern swept out into the main stream, leaving us little rope to hang on to.

Charlie screamed at me to tie my line off to a nearby tree. The tree in question was more than a metre from the end of my outstretched arm; and I, close to the end of the rope, had no more slack. John held the final few centimetres as tightly as he could with both hands. The tree was beyond his grasp, as well. There was nothing we could do to reach that or any other tree strong enough to anchor the boat. Neither of us had enough rope to get any purchase at all. The crew on the lines farther forward, out of our sight and unaware of our predicament, kept tight hold.

"I can't reach it!" I roared back at Charlie.

"We can't hold it! We can't hold it!" John added his voice to the shouts as the thick line burned into our hands. With that, he and I let go in a single motion. It was either let go or be dragged into the river and down the rapids.

David and Edward, far younger and stronger than John and I, had no chance to save the situation. Their line was ripped from their hands, too. The York, helped by the wind, turned beam on to the current. For a moment it looked as though it might fetch up on the safety of the opposite bank where there was a low clearing. Instead, the stern swung in an arc past a miniature promontory of flat land, missing it by a fraction. With no more barriers to stop her, she hurtled sideways to the falls with four men on board. There was nothing Gordon's crew could do to save the situation. They let go to give Ken a chance to straighten his course and run the rapids as best he and his three shipmates could.

The wind and the current gave them no chance to get the bow pointing down the gorge. Seconds later, a dreadful crash and the sound of ruptured timbers rebounded off the rocks. The York stopped abruptly, jammed across a big rock at the top of the first fall, her long stub of a keel showing.

We flew through the bushes, ignoring all obstructions, intent on getting in place to help our companions to safety. Miraculously, they had all managed to stay on board. Murray, Wayne, and Ken climbed off the stern onto some rocks and, with the help of convenient branches, made their way to safety on the far bank. They were fortunate in that the sheer cliffs began a few metres downstream from the boat. In its precarious circumstances, the York now made an unsteady bridge from one side of the river to the other.

Disregarding advice to the contrary, the rest of the crew, except Gordon, scampered one at a time across the tenuous link to Ken. Charlie joined Gordon and me on the southeast side of the river where the bow was jammed into a narrow fissure in the cliff. The force of the current held the boat tightly against the rocks, squeezing her up on her port side. She rapidly filled with water: some flowing over the gunwales; some eddying back from the white waves; most of it gushing in through a large hole near the stern below the waterline.

The pressure of the water was such that, even with the thick oars as levers, we could not get her bow out of the crack. We had to take weight off her. Charlie tied the painter fast to a tree on our side and told Ken to wrap a stern line around another tree across the river. Gordon stepped on board, keeping low, and cautiously felt his way over to the baggage.

At least two oars had floated off with the current. My metal camera case, which contained three cameras, six lenses, and assorted photographic items of equal value, made buoyant by foam separators, floated inside the boat at an odd angle. Gordon passed it to me, river water streaming from its seams. I opened it, poured out the water, swore a few times and felt lucky to have kept a Nikon close at hand. The other cameras would not be of much use in their saturated condition.

Gordon picked up the crew's bags and threw them one by one to Charlie, who passed them back to me. Next came the food containers, a couple of chainsaws, sleeping bags, and tents. Murray's kit bag didn't quite make it. Gordon tossed it to Charlie. He failed to get a grip on it, the bottom touched the boat's stem and the bag fell away from Charlie's outstretched hand. To groans of dismay from Murray, his kit bag went floating off down the rapids.

Emptied of our freight and as full of water as she could be, we still couldn't budge the York. Preferring not to risk my neck by stumbling over the boat, I crossed the river by canoe, upstream some way, to set up a rope winch on the opposite bank.

Truck drivers used to shorten and tighten ropes by a simple system of wrapping the rope around and looping through its own coils. With the aid of a well-anchored tree, I thought I might be able to use the same idea to gradually shorten the rope and pull the bow clear. When I explained it to Charlie and Ken, they agreed it just might be effective.

It didn't work as planned. I had enough strong guys to haul on the rope. My trucker's hitch[2] held, but the thick manila rope couldn't handle the strain and stretched. The boat remained jammed across the river.

Charlie cut down a tree the thickness of his forearm and managed to prise it between the rock wall and the bow as a lever. He and Gordon pulled on it. They leaned on it. They dangled from it with all their weight. Nothing moved, although the lever bent only slightly. On our side we lent our combined strength to the task. Eleven powerful, determined men could do no more than shift the stern a fraction. We took a break while Ken surveyed the scene from our side and Charlie and Gordon conferred with him in shouts from the opposite rocks.

"Okay, boys. Let's try again." Ken picked up the rope and wrapped it round his massive shoulders as he spoke. We took the strain once more and leaned back. Heels dug in and slowly, a fraction at a time, we walked backwards. The rope could not have been tighter without snapping, but still the river refused to release the York.

"And again, boys," Ken grunted. We obeyed, finding that little extra power. It was enough. We dug our heels in harder, leaned back a little more, and held on tenaciously. Charlie and Gordon made a last gasp effort; the bow came free. They fell over. On the opposite bank, we fell over.

To a chorus of cheers from semi-recumbent river runners, the York's stern swung lazily through a ninety-degree arc, the bow drifting across the racing current to our side. We had done it. She was facing the wrong way, but being a double-ender, that did not matter. She was free, but getting her down the rest of Hell Gates's rapids would still be a problem.

Although we knew the rapids on the Hayes River as Hell Gates, on many maps and in many books they are known by a similar name. Robert Hood, as long ago as 1819, wrote of them as Hill Gates.[3] Perhaps that was the original name, although Hell Gates is, as we discovered, a far more appropriate description.

Ken O. took the canoe across to pick up Charlie and Gordon and to ferry all the baggage to our side: a time-consuming process. The rest of us scouted the route along the cliff to make sure there were no more surprises in store. There were more rocks in the main chute, but not enough to create a major hazard at this stage. The terraces of standing waves were not big enough to exert too much strain on a big boat. Filled as she was with water, the York was in no more danger: as long as we exercised great care handlining her down the chute.

Once Charlie and Gordon rejoined us, we attached lines to every available projection on the boat. The free ends went up the cliff to be held by willing hands. With every available crew member positioned at regular intervals along the cliff top, the York was reasonably assured of a safe descent.

Ken untied the knot holding the stern and she bobbed a little, her gunwales awash, almost reluctant to leave. She didn't stay that way for long. The river was still in control, even then. She lurched and came alive. The lines tightened as the turbulence swirled around the crippled boat, seeking to shatter her on the next waiting rock. With steady hands, we guided her down the rushing water, over the standing waves, past the projections, to a shallow pool.

Carrying such a volume of water meant she was soon aground. Wayne and Ryan waded out to her with buckets to bail her out, as others hauled her in to the safety of calm water and the protection of the riverbank. Ken patched the gaping hole with a thin sheet of plywood he had stowed under the foredeck for emergencies, and a tube of silicone. He also treated the obviously open seams adjacent to the hole with the same sticky substance.

I dried all my camera equipment as best I could[4] — carefully wiping each item with a cloth before placing it in the sun to dry. Once home again, I hoped to be able to salvage some pieces. None of the equipment in the case would be of any further use on this trip. I stripped the soaked films out of the cameras and wiped the insides dry. Gordon helped by squeezing all the moisture out of the sponge padding in the case and drying it carefully over the fire before replacing it.

Once every item was as dry as possible under the circumstances, I wrapped everything and sealed it against future damage. As an added precaution I added miniature packets of dessicated silicagel to each package to absorb any unseen moisture. The three wet films, useless now, I added to the fire. All exposed and unexposed films, still sealed in their plastic canisters, had survived intact. I stored them in Ziploc plastic bags and tucked them in my kit bag.

Gordon handed me his Polaroid camera and asked me if I could clean and dry it. I tried, but it never did work again. My new Nikon, which had been in a pouch in the back of the bush jacket I was wearing, still had the 35–105 millimetre autofocus lens attached. I was lucky to have retained the camera and that lens. It was, overall, the most adaptable. I could still do the photography part of my job efficiently.

Ben belatedly told us we should have handlined from the opposite side right from the start. No one commented. We had all figured that out by then. Once again we loaded as much as we each could carry and tramped through the woods to the boat. Getting down to it, burdened as we were, was not so easy. The rocks, as in so many places we stopped, were covered in a thin layer of moss that tended to break away easily.

"Be careful, Tony, it's very slippery," Ken McKay warned me. Two of the crew had already fallen and got soaked. I heeded the warning, but it didn't help much. Burdened as I was, I slipped, anyway, and ended up soaked to the waist again, my legs underneath the York. By that time my ribs were well on the mend. The sudden jarring, as I bounced over rocks and slammed against the boat's hull, could not have done the cure a lot of good. Soaked, suddenly cold, worn out, and feeling thoroughly miserable, I swore loudly and profanely.

At 8:00 p.m., or a little later, we re-embarked. I and a few others would have been happy to put up tents where we were and sleep the night away, but Ken felt otherwise and on we went, leaving the aptly named Hell Gates behind. Ken O. and Wayne went ahead in the canoe to retrieve the lost oars and look for Murray's kit bag. They found everything stuck in some reeds at the end of the canyon. Murray was thrilled to have his kit returned; not so happy to have it returned quite so wet.

The remaining kitchen chair stayed behind at Hell Gates. Hurled overboard by the crash, it had tackled part of the rapids alone, until stopped abruptly in midstream. Held upright tightly against a rock by the water's power, it was out of our reach. It wouldn't do the wilderness any good, but it definitely improved the boat's profile. Future travellers on this stretch of the river would see an empty chair and wonder how it got there. If they also followed our route over Robinson Portage they would find its identical twin. Another wilderness mystery.

After an hour we came on to Lake Opiminegoka. The two Kens left us to drift around in the darkness in the York boat, while they went in search of a habitable campsite in the canoe. It was cold and windy. We were all tired and hungry and getting rather irritable with each other. We did not enjoy ourselves that evening on the pitch-black waters of Opiminegoka.

Charlie told me one evening that, prior to the beginning of the expedition, he had talked at length with the crew about the need for tolerance. Knowing, from his experiences as a wilderness guide, that tempers tend to fray under stressful situations, he had cautioned against it. He warned them that we would all have to get along and would have to work together. His sensible words had obviously been taken to heart by each and every member of the expedition. Despite an occasional testiness, rarely did we hear voices raised in anger. Even on Opiminegoka, cold, tired, and hungry, each kept his temper in check.

Wandering around a lake in the darkness was not what we had in mind that night. A hot meal and a warm bed were far more to our liking. We put up the sail and shone a flashlight on it to help the two Kens locate us again as we drifted in circles. They found us eventually, close to 10:00 p.m., and guided us to the chosen spot. It was a good one, a traditional York boat site on a small island between the lake and the Hayes River.

CHAPTER 12
Sailing on Windy Lake

THE HEAVENS TOOK PITY ON us weary travellers that night. A magnificent display of northern lights rippled across the sky. Although I had been in the North many times, that was only the third time I had witnessed the phenomenon. Ever-changing streaks of eerie green and purple lights shimmered and danced around us for a long time. I stood on the shore of the Hayes River with Ken Ormand and together we watched nature's exhibitionism painting the dark canopy of night.

Northern lights, or aurora borealis,[1] are caused by electrical disturbances in the atmosphere. Sometimes the colours change rapidly as the luminous streamers ripple across the polar skies. In some instances the aurora can be one of the most staggeringly beautiful sights on earth.

Ken told me that the Cree elders, or grandfathers, say the northern lights are the spirits of the dead who have come back to see how the world and their relatives are doing. If that is so, their return is stunning in its beauty. Behind us and shielded by trees, in stark opposition to the harmony above, the generator growled noisily and the electric lights blazed unnecessarily brightly. Charlie joined us to watch the show, hearing Ken's Native description of the lights. I asked my two companions if they knew of any books written expressly about Cree legends. Neither of them could answer the question, but Charlie didn't think it was likely.

"Stories and legends are passed on by the Cree elders," he said. "Nothing is written. If you can remember the story, you have earned the right to pass it on to someone of your choice."

Later he spoke of his interest in the philosophy and wisdom of the elders. He told me he had spent many long nights sitting listening to their tales and reminiscences. His admiration and respect for their sagacity knew no bounds. I could easily visualize the young Cree brave sitting cross-legged at the feet of his tribal elders, totally enthralled by their words.

The majority of the crew slept in the open that night. Snug in their bedrolls and sleeping bags, with a tarpaulin underneath and one suspended from branches above them as shelter in case of rain. They chattered and laughed for a long time. It felt good to hear so many happy voices after such a trying day.

I made a few notes about the day, half-a-dozen pages of my notebook, and settled back to reflect on the ideas Charlie had planted in my mind. One day, I vowed, I would find out more about those ancient legends. They are among the original heritage of legends of the enormous country we proudly know as Canada. As such they are of the utmost importance to us all.

Seven-fifteen a.m., August 25, 1994, our ninth day since leaving Norway House and my wife's birthday. I wondered what she was doing that day in far-off Antwerp. As soon as he woke up, Ken checked the amount of water which had collected in the boat since we left Hell Gates. It was considerable. Enough to finally convince him we should haul her out and do something about the situation.

Decisions may have taken time to reach but, having got there, actions followed extremely quickly.

The chainsaws roared into life and ripped into trees to fashion another set of rollers. The campsite was ideal for this exercise. A casually sloping rock shelf reached to the water's edge. Hardly any lifting was required. For a change, we expended little energy in getting the York into the dry.

Once clear of the lake the extent of the boat's injuries became apparent. Long streamers of silicone, clinging to strands of hemp caulking, hung like dirty spaghetti from far too many seams. Ken tugged delicately at each streamer until it either came free or proved itself stuck fast. Those that remained attached he snipped off at the hull and then consigned the loose ends to the fire.

We broke out fresh tubes of silicone and re-caulked all the seams, without the benefit of fresh hemp and, hopefully, sealed them against the possibility of incoming river water. Ken's big patch showed no sign of having leaked at all. Waiting for the sticky mess to set, our thoughts turned to food, even though it was too early for lunch.

A few pike, caught two days before and kept in ice chests, topped the menu. Ken O. fried some cutlets, boiled a few others, and at least one was grilled over the open fire. We had newly baked bannock, tasty fresh fish, hot tea, and, very soon, full stomachs. A really healthy treat for all of us. For me, a great lover of all kinds of river and sea fish, the meal was the best I had savoured since leaving home.

Once we rolled the York back into her natural element, reloaded her and commenced rowing, it became patently clear we had stopped the majority of leaks. Some water still found its way in, but not enough to have one or two men permanently bailing. A bucket every hour or so would do nicely until the next portage.

A strong southerly wind was blowing that day, helping us along toward Windy Lake. Charlie told us there is a legend that if one points while crossing Windy Lake the wind will follow. He advised us all not to tempt fate. I felt that, as long as the wind followed from the desired direction, pointing could only be to our advantage.

On that last broad straight of the Hayes prior to reaching the lake, we ran twelve kilometres in one hour, under sail and with the current. Considering the oars were shipped the whole time, it was a fast run.

Midshipman Hood referred to this area as the Rabbit Ground.[2] Franklin thought it was an absurd name. There may have been rabbits on or close to the riverbanks but, if they were there, they stayed well hidden from our view.

While we sailed with the wind, the canoe went on ahead to wait at the lake. Ken and Ben saw another black bear, this one trying to break into an old log cabin by the riverside. We didn't see the bear. By the time we reached the lake it had vanished into the woods, or had succeeded in its efforts at burglary. Either way, it was probably scared enough by our intimidating approach to hide.

The Cree call Windy Lake *Notin Sakahigan.*[3] The voyageurs named it *Lac des Vents*[4] and told of it usually being windy and turbulent. On this day, Windy Lake looked as if it might live up to its name. As the only one on board with sailing experience, I took charge. I let the York drift while we tied the canoe alongside and brought the crew on board. Our rowers settled down out of the wind and Charlie took control of the steering sweep. The lake was fairly calm at first, but I could feel the wind veering to come in from the northwest. In the distance, a stretch of surf was visible as a milky, white line. I turned to Charlie and warned him we would almost certainly be hit by some hard gusts of wind as we passed a headland on our left.

Charlie nodded and flicked a glance at the potential trouble spot. Wayne looked up at the full sail, then at me, and drew his sheath knife. He indicated the sail and port halyard. I shook my head.

"Don't do anything unless I tell you."

Gordon prepared himself in the same fashion by the other halyard.

Library and Archives Canada/PA-041509.

A fleet of York boats under sail, with oars at rest. When the wind was blowing from the right direction, sailing was a convenient way for the tripmen to take a rest while the boats kept moving.

Out on the lake, beyond the headland, whitecaps danced in extravagant chorus lines: the surf I had seen earlier. The wind kicked the waves up to close to a metre in height. For a moment I debated whether to pull in to shore for a tea break and wait until the wind subsided. Waiting for calmer conditions, however, could take a few days. We kept going. There was no modern Ulysses to lead us; no great quest to define our limited odyssey. Our inspiration was the fur trade, and our own sense of adventure. Even so, Homer's magical lines related well to the day's task:

> The chief his orders gives; the obedient band with due observance wait the chief's command; with speed the mast they rear, with speed unbind the spacious sheet, and stretch it to the wind. High o'er the roaring waves the spreading sails bow the tall mast, and swell before the gales …[5]

Our initial course put us beam on to the wind and the waves. I looked at Charlie anxiously and warned him we were in for a rough ride.

"Can you hold that sweep all right?"

He nodded, his silent reply amplified by the way he curled his fingers around the hand grips and braced his legs on the deck.

The York really seemed to enjoy the sudden action as she bounced over the first few swells and crashed through others. With the headland astern, she heeled over wildly as the first gust attacked, hard on the port beam. The starboard rail dipped alarmingly close to the lake's disturbed surface. Wayne and Gordon watched me, knives poised. I shook my head.

"Take her downwind, now," I yelled at Charlie, pointing and forgetting the legend. "That way," I yelled again to emphasize the order, my arm outstretched and finger aimed like a pistol.

"Don't point!" A chorus of concerned voices clamoured.

Charlie pushed hard on the steering sweep, turning the York a few degrees to starboard. She came back up, almost on an even keel again. The waves slammed into the stern, parted, and raced along each side, lifting the canoe to our level as they passed. The wind stretched the square red sail to its fullest extent as the York proved it really was a sailor. We relaxed a little.

I have sailed on many kinds of yachts as well as square-rigged sailing ships on lakes and seas around the world. The mighty windjammers of the Russian and Ukrainian marine academies had been an important part of my nautical training less than three years before. Sailing a heavy, almost keel-less[6] York boat in high winds on a choppy lake, with a primitive square rig and fixed halyards, was quite another matter.

I pointed at Charlie, then to the left of an island, without dissent from the crew this time. Charlie altered course a little. The York heeled over a few degrees, but not enough to cause concern. I watched for a few minutes to make sure we could handle the strain.

A quick glance up at Charlie and an exuberant pair of thumbs stuck up in the air earned me a huge smile.

We were sailing as efficiently as we could under the circumstances. Without a full keel, and with loose freight on board, I didn't want to risk capsizing. The lack of life jackets kept popping into my mind. I brushed the thought aside and concentrated on the job at hand.

On the aft deck, his shiny black ponytail flapping in the wind, Charlie was in his element. I sat close by, my feet braced against a food chest. My eyes roamed from the whitecaps to the sail, from the sail to Charlie. The wind was getting stronger, the waves a little bigger. We began to wallow in the troughs. As we slid off the waves, Charlie fought to keep her on an even keel. If the wind turned us broadside on to the waves, without the stabilizing effect of a keel, she would roll for sure. In that event we would be swimming and our equipment would be on the bottom of the lake. Charlie proved to be a natural sailor. He kept his eyes on me and followed my course corrections without hesitation. His immense strength kept us on track and out of trouble.

The long steering sweep wasn't really designed for those conditions. A heavy rudder would have been of great benefit that day. Many of the fur-trade York boats did carry rudders.[7] They were mounted solely for the purpose of crossing large, open bodies of water, such as Windy Lake, under sail. As we came within hailing distance of a group of small islands I tugged on the starboard halyard. It was as taut as a bowstring.

"Ease her over to the left a fraction, Charlie."

He moved the sweep, his eyes fixed on me.

"A little more, Charlie. You're doing great."

Charlie flinched as the boat took a big wave over the afterdeck. The water ran over his feet and my legs to disappear in the bilge. As we closed the islands the chop was shorter and harder. We bounced along with our lee rail skimming just above the surface. For a few anxious moments we angled across the waves. The York would have

Glenbow Museum Archives/NA-1847-5.

A York boat under sail en route to Oxford House for the Hudson's Bay Company in the 1880s.

been a magnificent sight from a few boat lengths away. Sail full, bow alternately lifting and plunging, waves building high above her stern; Charlie, standing proud with the steering sweep. Once more I signalled a correction. Charlie took her downwind a little and she righted herself again.

Our exit from the lake, back onto the Hayes River, was to the north of our position. With the wind as it was, there was no possibility of sailing in that direction. York boats are not designed for tacking into and across the wind. Charlie and I got her as close to the river as we could. In the lee of a small islet covered in trees, almost across the lake, with the wind blocked, I furled the sail. Charlie let go of the steering sweep and stretched his cramped arm and shoulder muscles. His smile showed how much he had enjoyed handling the boat under sail.

We set the canoe adrift with its crew and Ken took over the steering again, calling for the oars to take us the last hundred metres — hard into the wind — to the river. We had crossed the lake in one hour, a distance of eight kilometres by our course. It had been an exhilarating though nerve-racking sixty minutes, for two of us at least.

Back on the river there was no time to rest. We soon found ourselves on the brink of more rapids. The first one, called *Hahasew*, was a pleasure cruise. Without hesitation we lined the York up with the main flow and she ran through the crest with all on board. Spray flew over the bow as she ploughed through the whitewater, bow down and stern high in the air. We made it safely, with Gordon directing operations from the bow. A few seconds later the canoe followed in our wake.

That part of the Hayes River, which eventually connects Windy Lake with Oxford Lake, used to be called the Wipanipanis River. It is less than ten kilometres in length. The first two-thirds is a stepladder of rapids leading down to a waterfall. None of the rapids were particularly dangerous for us. There wasn't enough water running over the rocks for that, they were simply time-consuming.

At Moore Rapids we scouted from shore, taking advantage of a large patch of wild cranberries for a quick and healthy snack. I knew that, in 1818, a tripman had drowned while handlining a boat upstream through this rapid.[8] It was a sobering thought, which I kept to myself as we studied the options. The most sensible route, that with the deepest water and least turbulence, flowed by the west bank. We were on the east bank with a clear passage across to the west bank, where a large pool stood in front of the initial drop. The crossing was a matter of pushing off from one bank, a couple of deep thrusts with the oars and a steering correction. Unloading was not necessary. The crew jumped ashore and took hold of the long lines. Handlining (by that time we were getting skilled at the art) took the York down in a few moments. Ken and Charlie stayed on board to keep the boat in position with the two steering oars.

We handled Seeseep Rapids, the next drop, in much the same way, though we had a doubt or two about the narrow passage through the granite-lined channel. It was a tight squeeze but, with two men on board and the York close enough for those of us on land to hold the gunwales if necessary, she bobbed through like a huge black cork.

Out of Seeseep we entered a sizeable pool with two obvious wide exits. Without the advantage of the topographical maps — still sitting on Ken's desk at Norway House — we had to guess at the correct stream. The York took the right-hand fork. The canoe, with me and Ken O. on board, followed. A hundred metres along I had a feeling we might have taken the wrong fork and suggested to Ken that we try the other one.

Ken turned us 180 degrees and we went exploring. The York continued merrily on its way in the opposite direction. A short time later we saw another stream joining our river from the right. We knew the York was on it — we could hear the rumble of the oars. And there it was, aiming straight at us. As we passed the opening, the York's rowers were thrashing the water to foam, trying to catch us. Ken McKay had already figured, correctly, that he was circling an island.

By 4:45 p.m. we were perched on a rocky shelf in the sunshine. Ken O. had a fire beginning to blaze and we had food and drink on our minds. Charlie and Gordon took the canoe to examine the next rapid and Wipanipanis, the waterfall beyond. Unfortunately for us, they took the food, plates, and mugs with them. There were no snacks and no tea or coffee for us that afternoon. As the distance to the next potential trouble spot could not be far, we were all willing to wait a while longer for our break.

We extinguished the unused fire, the rowers picked up their oars, and we pushed away from the rock. Charlie normally acted as lead rower, setting the pace. Occasionally he and Ken McKay would trade places as Ken also enjoyed rowing. In Charlie's absence, however, Wayne took his oar and I took Wayne's, right behind him. The sun was bright; the sky clear. The air was warm. On either side the land was fairly flat, covered in tall grass waving lazily in the breeze.

Occasional trees broke up the regularity of the riverbanks. Charlie and Gordon came back, swinging in a tight circle round our stern. Ken McKay called for more effort.

"Aha, boys!"

He started the well-known litany and we responded. Charlie urged us on with shouts of encouragement. We cleared a small, unnamed rapid without a break in the rowers' rhythm. Signs of man were beginning to intrude around us. A steel post and two or three wooden ones stood upright in the river to our left. They served no immediately apparent purpose. With my back to the future and my eyes on the past, I couldn't see the obstruction I knew had to be somewhere in front of the boat. I kept rowing in time with Wayne's oar. After a while Ken steered us to the west bank. I could hear the sound of rushing water and knew it had to be the beginning of the waterfall. That meant we had reached the winter road.

Ken ordered the oars shipped and turned the York into a sheltered bay. We stood up, stretched tired muscles, and stepped ashore. Man's work was right beside us. We tied up to layers of carefully levelled rocks. The gaps between had been filled with smaller rocks and gravel. This was the winter road and, stretching across the river, the ugly and modern winter road bridge.

Standing on the substantial gravel road, I strolled over to look at the latest impediment to our progress. A bridge of iron girders spanned the river. Directly underneath it the water dropped in a dead fall over a metre to the subsequent level. The flow was fast and exhausted itself on boulders, as usual. We checked the height between the water level and the underside of the bridge. We measured the York from the shallow keel to the top of the stern steering post. It would not fit under the bridge.

CHAPTER 13
The Wreck at Wipanipanis Falls

WHILE KEN PONDERED THE PROBLEM, a group of us crossed the bridge to study the falls. There was a resemblance to Sea River Falls, our first rapid descent on Day 1 of the expedition. This one, named Wipanipanis Falls, was wider than the Sea River chute, but would not be navigable. The ledges over which the torrent raced were too sharp and too clearly defined for our use. On the far side of the falls we could see a possible portage link. That would have to be explored later. Franklin referred to this site as Swampy Portage.[1] Two of the boats with his party suffered damage here by being dashed against the rocks and had to be repaired. I hoped that was not an omen for us.

Wipanipanis is said to mean "the angling, or fishing place."[2] It looked a perfect spot for a little casting, but we had other work to do first.

Back at the York we could all see a natural portage route, or it could have been man-made, to circumvent the bridge. A gentle, flat ramp led parallel to the road, leading away from the bridge. It crossed the road at right angles, made another right angle turn, and slid meekly back to the river again. With the York emptied and a few rollers cut, that portage should have been the least bothersome to date. The reality was that the expedition came to an unexpected and unnecessarily premature end at the winter road bridge crossing. We did manage to travel a little farther, but only out of necessity.

The winter road is precisely what it says. A road that can only be used by wheeled or track vehicles once the ice and snow of winter have frozen the land. Travel at any other time of the year would encounter major problems, the abundant river crossings being high on the list.

The ruins of a burned-out building scarred the beauty of the setting even more than the ugly bridge. Charlie told me that someone had tried to open a small motel and restaurant on that spot. Residents of communities at each end of the winter road had violently objected to the commerce, interpreting it as a threat to their own livelihood. The wreckage stood as a reminder of mankind's greed and distrust when faced with competition.

Whitewater over the main cataract at Wipanipanis Falls. Taking the York boat down this turbulence was never an option.

So many York boats and canoes have journeyed up and down this historic river. So many men, Cree, Métis, and Europeans have camped on its timeless banks. Wipanipanis Falls is a delightful location. It's an ideal camping site with plenty of room for a flotilla of York boats. I could easily imagine explorers like Franklin, Hood, Back, Dr. John Rae, and countless others, writing their journals within hearing of the falls. For them and all the others who laboured on this important trade route, there was no winter road bridge to scar the landscape or to impede their progress.

Though the modern bridge was a barrier to our movement on the river, the obvious portage route close by showed we could get the boat around the iron structure without too much effort. Inexplicably, Ken suggested he cut the sternpost down so the boat would fit under the bridge. I argued that to do so would immediately remove his steering position. My words fell on deaf ears. Ken then talked about filling the boat with water to reduce its profile so it would fit under the bridge. A chorus of complaints from half-a-dozen or more voices greeted this idea. The majority wanted to portage the boat as the only realistic option and the safest way to proceed.

The discussion ranged back and forth in Cree, some voices raised in what sounded like anger. Eventually, the crew voted. There were two choices open: take the portage, or sink the boat and float it under the bridge? My lack of a vote didn't matter. Most of the crew agreed with me that the portage was the best plan. The vote was eight to four against sinking the York and floating it down.

On this occasion, democracy was not given a chance. Ken elected to ignore the count and condemned his boat to be temporarily sunk. Gordon unstepped the mast while a disgruntled crew emptied the boat of all baggage before filling her with water. I noted in my journal "… If this goes wrong, and I think it will, we have a long walk ahead of us."

The crew lined the bridge, looking down on the route the boat would take. None of them looked happy. With no real choice in the matter, other than outright mutiny, we took hold of the lines as Ken ordered and coaxed the York to turn sluggishly into the current. At first the boat hesitated, the weight of water inside her hull holding her back. When she decided to run it was sudden and sensational.

The current caught the bow, dragging the sad-looking semi-submerged boat with it. The stern drifted out into the stream. The bow dropped under the bridge. The loose and volatile cargo of water raced to the bow as predicted. The stern kicked up like a bucking bronco and it was over. A crack, which should have been audible in Oxford House, shattered the wilderness.

The York was trapped under the bridge, her steering post stripped almost completely from the stern. No one bothered to say "I told you so" to Ken. Some looked at me questioningly, expecting

As the York boat raced under the winter road bridge at Wipanipanis Falls, the impact ripped the sternpost out of the boat.

© Anthony Dalton Collection

me to comment. I shrugged my shoulders and leaned back against the bridge with my eyes closed. I had nothing more to say. My disappointment must have been emblazoned on my face, adding colour to my anger. The expedition we had put so much effort into had been jeopardized by an unpopular and foolish manoeuvre.

Buffeted by the rushing waters of the Hayes River, the York boat was trapped. The current tried to force her under the bridge to be swept to the merciless falls on the right. The sternpost, still holding on by a few strong wooden fibres, and the aft deck, kept the boat wedged tightly under the bridge. Filled with water as she was, we couldn't pull her back. There was no choice left; she would have to continue her rough passage. Ryan climbed over the bridge and carefully dropped onto the boat to tie a fresh painter on the bow. He threw the loose end to Charlie and scrambled back onto the bridge. While we watched, expecting the boat to break up at any moment, Ken took an axe and gave the shattered sternpost a hefty smack with the blunt head.

The boat lurched and bucked. The blow, ripping more of the sternpost away, enabled the current to take hold. The York groaned, as if in agony, then scraped painfully out from under the bridge. Bow down, she slammed into the lower level of water. To the right the river sped toward the waterfall. To the left, by the bank, it was calm. Before she could respond to the river's pressure and turn to her destruction at the falls, eager crew pulled her close to shore by the painter. And there she stopped, her steering position hanging almost to the water and her rear dangerously exposed. I was surprised the hull planking hadn't sprung. She was a sad and sorry sight.

Night was falling as Charlie tied the battered York safely to a tree. There was little we could do for her in the dark, even with the aid of the generator and lights. I was angry with Ken for taking such a pointless chance against the wishes of most of us. With the York in its severely damaged condition, and a lot of wild rapids ahead, not to mention some notoriously choppy lakes, to go on with the expedition could result in one or more of us getting seriously injured or worse. Ken came over to where I sat writing the saga and told me he would get the boat fixed the next day. He was only too aware that I, among others, was far from happy with the day's events.

Keeping my voice low, I expressed my doubts about his leadership abilities, and about the strength of the boat as it then stood. I just could not understand how someone could build a boat with such skill and then not look after it. The only way the expedition had any chance of success, I told Ken, was with a seaworthy boat. Our York was far from safe and he didn't seem interested in keeping up the repairs. I added that I would think about leaving in the morning. Four of the crew had, without knowing of my decision, announced that they too wanted to go home.

Later, Gordon talked with me for a while. Ken had told him what I said and, I assumed, asked him to reason with me. Gordon told me he was not happy that I planned to leave. I wasn't happy, either, and said so, explaining why in detail. A great deal of time and effort had gone into the expedition. I was as keen as the rest to be on board the York boat when it reached York Factory. *If* it reached York Factory.

I have never been averse to taking risks. However, my risk-taking escapades in the past have been calculated and based on my own known abilities. I didn't see much sense in risking my neck any further when I had no control over events. Had Charlie taken over the leadership, I believe the expedition would have stood a reasonable chance of success. I kept the thought to myself. I didn't believe I had the right to initiate that course of action. Although we had been together through the rough and the smooth, I was still, to some extent, the outsider. We had the most peaceful meal of the expedition so far that night. There was an air of gloom over the camp. Little conversation interrupted the repast. Each was busy with his own thoughts.

CHAPTER 14
An End, and a New Beginning

A T DAYBREAK KEN AND GORDON nailed the sternpost back on, cementing it in place with a thick bed of silicone. Privately, I was convinced the strenuous movements of the steering oar would eventually show up the weakness and the sternpost would fall apart again. As York boats are essentially double-enders,[1] I suggested turning the boat around and using the undamaged stem as the sternpost until we reached Oxford House. My idea was ignored.

With five of us prepared to leave the expedition, Charlie unpacked the radio for the first time. We strung a long antenna from the top of a tree and stretched it out as far as it would go at the end of a long, thin pole. Hoping to get a float plane to come in and pick us up from a convenient landing space north of the falls, he tried for about fifteen minutes without success. Perhaps the proximity of the iron bridge interfered with the signals. Not having any alternative, even though the boat was in sad shape, we had to keep going for a while longer.

Charlie and I walked through the bushes bordering the west bank of the river to find the simplest way to get the York over the falls without any more damage. The main falls, we noted, were separated from a smaller drop by an island of flat granite with a few bushes on top. We studied both sides of the island, quickly rejecting the one closest to the bridge as too difficult. Instead, there was a usable route, one we had seen the day before, on the far side of the cataract. There, shallow, slow-moving water ran over a number of barely visible ridges on that side.

Charlie waded into the knee-deep water, testing the rocks. He cautioned that it was very slippery underfoot, but a workable route. We went back and reported the find. The crew set to work immediately. While half the crew ferried all our baggage to the island by canoe and portaged it to the north side, the others carefully rowed the York around a small bay close to shore, away from the main waterfall.

It was a struggle to get the boat, even empty as it was, over some of the ledges. But, by then, all of us knew exactly what to do to keep the boat moving. We waded in the water beside her, guiding her along the deepest course, taking care not to slip, and lifting her by brute strength when necessary. It didn't take long to get her bow up onto the shelving rock of the low-lying island. With the help of a few log rollers, and a lot of grunting and heaving, she rolled smoothly out of the water, without incident, to be left to dry out on the smooth sunny granite.

Once again the caulking was hanging in dirty white streamers. Wayne peeled the long strands of silicone away and cut them off. Until the hull dried out there wasn't much anyone could do to effect repairs. Ryan went fishing. The canoe team prepared lunch. Others went to sleep. Charlie, Ken, Gordon, and Wayne stayed beside the vessel. I found a comfortable place to sit and started writing.

Wayne got busy caulking as soon as he could, trying to seal as many seams as possible before she went back in the water. I heard hammering and sawing and wondered about it briefly, but paid little attention. Assuming the carpentry was to our benefit, I carried on with my notes.

Two men drew up in a motorboat. They were from Oxford House and travelling upriver on a hunting expedition. Intent on reaching their destination, the two didn't stay long. Before they left they said they would be passing again in a couple of days. They also told us there were some fishermen off the point at the entrance to Oxford Lake.

After the hunters left, Charlie came to talk, bending down to where I sat writing.

"I think you should look at something," he said, obviously concerned. He straightened and turned back to the York. I closed my notebook, stood up, and followed. Wayne was busy caulking by the keel. He wriggled out from under the hull as we reached him. Charlie pointed at the keel where Wayne had been working. I knelt on the rock and ran my fingers lightly over the part of the keel Charlie had indicated.

About one-third of the distance along the keel from the bow there was a crack. Not just a hairline fracture of the wood. The keel had snapped right through, though the planking around it looked and felt intact. There was no way of knowing when it had happened, perhaps as far back as Robinson Falls, or at Hell Gates. Only the day before, most likely. I looked inside the hull to see if any cracks were visible there. What I saw worried me. Directly over the keel, running the length of the boat and securely attached to the ribs, was a plank, called a keelson.[2] Two weak points were terribly apparent.

On one side of the keel crack location there was a butt join in the keelson. I had never been happy about that join: if used at all, it should have been scarfed for greater strength. A single long plank with no joins would have been eminently preferable. The keelson now caused me even greater concern. On the other side of the join, for some indeterminate reason, a piece of the keelson about thirty centimetres long had been cut out. That piece had been cut out during that morning. There was still sawdust in the boat and the edges of the remaining lengths of the keelson were rough and dry. As the crew gathered, I expressed my fears about this new problem. Ken said he would repair the boat at Oxford House. Unfortunately, this lack of consideration for common sense safety procedures created an unavoidable schism.

My disappointment at the events of the previous day, combined with this latest concern stretched my temper to the limit. Taking a deep breath and trying to keep the anger off my face and out of my voice, I leaned against the boat and addressed the crew. There was no doubt in anyone's mind that I was far from happy. After explaining the danger inherent in a weak keel, I reminded everyone that Oxford Lake was only a short distance ahead and it had a reputation for windy conditions and rough water. Only a couple of days before, Windy Lake had been a test for the boat and crew. We had survived that test, but now the equation had changed. Then we had no knowledge of the weakness in the keel, if in fact it was already damaged by then. Now we did. And with that knowledge, the lack of life jackets became an extremely important issue. A seriously damaged boat, no life jackets, and some non-swimmers added up to a disaster waiting to happen.

Wayne mused on the need for a couple of the thin, metal rails from Robinson Portage.

"One down each side of the keel would hold it, wouldn't it?" he asked me.

"Sure. Two lengths and some thick bolts would solve the problem forever, but we don't have them here."

I walked away then to let them discuss the situation among themselves. Deep down I knew I was right and I was sure most of the crew understood that fact. I had a feeling of being crippled, with no control over events. It was an unusual experience for me; one I didn't enjoy at all. We could afford a delay of a few days while the canoe team went to Oxford House to find the materials we needed. Taking the boat out on the lake made little or no sense. Going any farther without adequate repairs had the look of a suicide mission.

While the Cree talked through the problem in their own language, I looked at a moose skull that sat bleaching on the rock. Whether the beast had died from natural causes or from a hunter's bullet was not apparent. I removed a couple of teeth and kept them as souvenirs.

When I rejoined the crew, they were preparing to relaunch the boat. Obviously the decision had been made, despite the potential danger. Wayne showed me where he had nailed short planks of wood with bevelled ends on each side of the keel, across the break. Insignificant though the gesture was, it could only be a help. Only later did it occur to me that those two pieces of wood had come from the interior plank: the all-important keelson. That was why it had been cut, in a rather weak attempt to strengthen the keel.

As gently as possible, we rolled the York a few more metres over the island and into the water. As everything was reloaded I made sure the weight was well aft of the weak points, the only protection I could think of. We had less than four kilometres of calm water to row, with low-lying swampland on either side of us, before we reached the lake. I'm certain that many of us were expecting to go for a swim at any time.

Ken took the boat on to the lake, keeping close to the shore toward Seekowsueenik Point. The fishermen we had been told about were no longer there. None of the rowers exerted themselves. An air of extreme caution hung over the silent crew. As the fishermen had gone, Ken then angled the boat across to the opposing shore, crossing a kilometre of smooth, open water safely. There was no possibility of getting ashore there, so he crossed back to a few boat lengths from the other side again. I asked why take such a risk? But my question was ignored.

The rowers stopped and rested their oars, awaiting orders. None came, just a flick of the captain's head. The oarsmen began pulling again. The lake was calm; even so, I took note of the shortest swimming route to shore with reasonable access to dry land, in case we needed it suddenly. Every creak and groan from the hull was amplified in my mind. Every ripple flowing under the hull took on the appearance of the wave that would finally sink us. Once I saw Wayne make the sign of the cross. Throughout that long afternoon I was acutely aware of the lack of life jackets on board.

Nine kilometres passed and we approached a headland named Omaseesokwapa Point. Some distance before the promontory was a sheltered site flat enough for us to go ashore for a brew. From there we could see that, beyond the point, the lake was open and had an unhealthy-looking chop building up. We went ashore for tea and another talk. Ken asked me if I wanted to go on ahead with Ken Ormand in the canoe to Oxford House to get help. I declined the offer. I was determined to keep the York boat in sight for as long as necessary to forestall any attempt at pointless heroics by any member of the crew. Ryan offered to go with the canoe. The distance was thirty-five kilometres as the crow flies, more on the island-hopping route they would have to take to stay out of the wind.

The canoe left immediately, hugging the shore. They would have a rough time crossing the westerly wind to Kisetpiskanak Island and on to Carghill Island. We followed, rowing slowly up to the lea of the point, also keeping close in. There we would stay until Ken and Ryan returned with another boat or two.

Charlie and I went tramping through the woods to see if there was a better campsite anywhere. We both enjoyed the ramble, restricting our conversation to a discussion of the beauty of the forest. After a while we found a better site along the shore. Although it smelled like a decaying fish market, it had much better protection from the wind for the York. Cats would have loved that place. Fishermen had cleaned and gutted a lot of fish on the flat rocks at the water's edge. The gulls had picked the bones clean and the sun and wind had dried them. Nothing had erased the smell. Among the trees, a few metres inland from the lake, a small clearing with a thick bed of moss offered a respectable campsite. The site was almost ideal for our use. Once again we moved the York. This time across a bay sheltered from the wind.

We collected dead wood and soon had a fire at the water's edge. We fuelled it by the addition of the grinning skulls and carcasses of meatless northern pike. The plan was to keep a big fire burning all night so that Ken and Ryan could find us if they got back before dawn. No one really expected to see them until well into the following day. Most of us were content to be on shore and wait in safety.

I went wandering in the woods, desperate to be alone for a while. As I walked I thought about the repairs needed to get the boat back into serviceable condition. The broken keel could be bolted back together with the help of a couple of long, galvanized steel plates — one on each side, as Wayne had suggested. The keelson and the sternpost had to be completely replaced and the hull needed major re-caulking. All of it was possible, and not difficult to achieve, though time was against us. The major problem, as I saw it, was that I did not understand the Cree culture and so could not effectively guess what decisions might be made.

Far from the camp it was peaceful, only occasionally would a shout reach my ears. For nearly an hour I ranged in a wide circle, kneeling to look closely at unfamiliar plants and to admire unknown creatures. A furry caterpillar, the larva of a Tussock Moth (*Orgyia pseudotsugata*), marched purposefully along a twig laying flat on a smooth rock. The caterpillar was about two centimetres long with two black stripes bordering a yellow central band. I studied it for a while, noting it appeared to have identical ends, each decorated with a crown of long, white whiskers. When it reached the end of the twig I half expected it to go into reverse and retrace its steps, but it didn't. Gracefully, the successive rows of miniature legs glided daintily from twig to stone and promenaded away. I nicknamed it "Echimamish" because, like the river of the same name, it looked like it could go both ways.

On the way back to the lakeside I collected an armful of logs for the fire. If we were going to have a beacon it seemed a good idea to have a big one. Other crew members had been collecting, too. As darkness fell, the flames crackled and roared through the dry wood, sending sparks rocketing into the night sky. For a while we fed the hungry blaze, standing close and enjoying the intense heat. Once again, as at Wipanipanis Falls, conversation was limited.

When I was a young boy at scout camp, I used to sit for hours staring into the campfire. The other scouts would laugh and accuse me of homesickness. I denied it, even though they were probably right. My grandfather had taught me to watch for recognizable shapes in the flames and burning embers of a coal fire. As a scout I had done the same with a log fire. In my years as an expedition leader I often studied the fire without being aware of why I did it. Probably I had always looked for something that wasn't really there. That night I sat on the flat granite, stared into the wild furnace and imagined I could see home. When tiredness overtook us, most of us chose to sleep in the open that night.

Well before dawn, when the sky was still black and the only light was the bright red heat from the subsiding embers of our fire, I heard voices. Ken and Ryan were back with another man. I hadn't heard an outboard motor, neither had anybody else. Without warning the three stood looking down at our slumbering forms.

"Where's Ken?" A voice asked.

I drowsily indicated the collection of bodies over to my left. The sleeping bags and bed rolls began to wriggle like a collection of gigantic coloured maggots. Yawns and muffled questions filled the air as tired tripmen scratched themselves and tried to wake up. Over hastily brewed coffee we sat around the rekindled fire and talked.

Ken Ormand told us it was really windy out on the lake and he'd found it difficult, though not impossible, to keep the canoe upright. Despite the conditions, his skill had got them safely to their destination. Knowing neither of them had life jackets, I could easily imagine the potential for a capsize and its attendant risks. I had once been rolled over in a small boat by a big wave off the northwest coast of Arctic Alaska.[3] Clinging to an upturned boat in a storm, trying to stay alive, one is well aware of the proximity of death. Even wearing a life jacket and a floatation suit it had been a frightening experience for me. Without the safety clothing I would have died: just as many of the inhabitants in the cemetery at Norway House had met their end.

We learned that a few other boats should be coming out from Oxford House to escort us in sometime during the morning. We didn't wait for them to reach us. For the final sector across Oxford Lake, and at Ken's request, I travelled in the motor boat with the newcomer and Ben. We would keep station within sight of the York in case of trouble. It was cold in that little boat that morning. The sky was overcast and the dawn wind was chilly. For the first time, I sat and talked with Ben on a one-to-one basis. He told me about the poetry he wrote; the first I had heard of his talents in the literary field. He said he had been published a few times without earning much money from his craft. Ben had no great illusions of fame and fortune. He just wanted to see his work in print more often. I promised to send him addresses of Canadian and American publishers who looked favourably on poets.

We stopped for morning tea and coffee on an island. There the York boat crew took advantage of the break to have a wash and brush up.

"There's girls at Oxford House," one of them explained with a big grin on his face. The younger guys shaved off wisps of beard and trimmed their moustaches. They crouched on the rocks, leaned over the water and scrubbed their bodies clean before unpacking fresh shirts. Enthusiastically, they made ready for their arrival at Oxford House.

Having talked with Charlie about the Cree belief in the wisdom of the elders, I was all the more convinced they would advise against going on to York Factory this year. I started thinking about going home as soon as possible and said so. No one was surprised. I think they all knew that Oxford House would see the termination of the expedition for 1994, perhaps forever.

Back on the lake we passed a long island, almost completely barren of trees. In comparison to the others we had passed, it looked as if it had been the victim of a tornado attack. Ben said it was where the Oxford House people got their firewood. I hoped someone, perhaps the all-wise community elders, had thought to replant for the future.

Two other motorboats appeared in the distance. Off to their left another one was speeding on a course to pass well away from the York. We changed course slightly and headed directly to yet another island, which we reached shortly after the two motorboats from Oxford House. The York, still under muscle power, cruised along in our wake. The lake, known for its ability to change from flat calm to short, choppy waves in a matter of minutes, remained placid for us. The slight wind of the early morning had all but died.

Our short stay on that rocky outcrop of an island was to be the last time I was close to the York boat that summer. It was also the last time I saw the crew. We had more liquids and dry bannock. The sun was hot and the sky clear and blue by early afternoon. I spread my body out in a natural hollow in the rocks and soaked up the sun. I wanted to go home and I wanted to stay with the York. Had there been any chance of quick and effective repairs at Oxford House, my choice would have been easy. I was sure, and Ben confirmed it, there was little likelihood of such an eventuality.

The weather had been kind to us for the past few weeks, and there was every indication the trend would continue for some days to come. It was unlikely to last for much longer. Next year, even if the boat was seaworthy, we might not be so fortunate with the elements. While I pondered the situation our York boat crew sat around and talked with the new Cree arrivals. One of the guys from Oxford House told me there would be a plane in on its way to Winnipeg later that afternoon. Convinced the York was destined to spend the winter at Oxford House, I made my decision. I was ready to leave.

The York continued with its escort to a reed-choked passage that heralded the approach to Back Lake and beyond to the continuation of the Hayes River. As we separated, I waved farewell to the crew, seeing a few arms raised in return.

Less than half an hour later I was dropped off at a rickety wooden dock behind a gasoline station. That was the closest I could be taken to the airstrip. I shook hands with my two companions and told Ben I would send him some publishing addresses. With my heavy pack on my back and camera bag in hand I set off on foot. At the first dusty intersection a van pulled up and the driver offered me a lift. I accepted willingly.

With time to kill before my flight, I walked to the end of the runway. It was not far, a hundred metres or so. From there a gravel road led off into the bush. Beside it a large sign warned of the dangers of travelling the winter road route without proper preparations. Had I been able to follow the track that day, I would have eventually come to the iron bridge across the Hayes River. The same bridge that had effectively finished our river journey for that year.

When the little prop-jet landed, it used the full length of the runway, spun in a tight circle, and taxied to the apron. With engines howling and the two propellers sending dust flying in all directions, it lurched to a halt in front of the terminal building. Fifteen minutes later I was on board as we raced down the runway, screamed over the trees, and banked over Oxford House. The lake was spread out below for a few seconds, but I couldn't see the York boat. Southwards we turned, over the forests of firs, on course for Winnipeg, and, within a few days, home.

Soon after I arrived home I received confirmation that the elders had indeed stopped the expedition in Oxford House. The York boat, I was told, would stay put until the following spring when it would get a complete overhaul. Already I was mentally preparing myself for a second summer on the Hayes River with the Cree. We had worked too hard together to quit halfway. The coming winter would be a good opportunity to get myself really fit for the next stage of the river journey.

In September I mailed Charlie a slim book on the basics of sailing. Knowing his interest in the subject, and mindful of the potential for sailing the York on more lakes the next summer, it seemed appropriate. Having two sailors on board would be an advantage on Knee Lake, Swampy Lake, and the final long run after the rapids to York Factory, the mouth of the Hayes River and Hudson Bay.

At the end of February, Ken McKay phoned. He and the boys had discussed the future of the expedition and decided to have another go. He said the crew would be having another meeting in Norway House the following week during which my involvement would be discussed. Ken went on to say that the planned departure would be June 12. He said he intended going to Oxford House with two of the crew for the last week in May to completely overhaul the York. I assured him I would keep June and July free.

Ken phoned again at Easter, to wish me "Happy Easter" and to let me know I was definitely invited to be part of the team again. I felt sure that Charlie and Wayne had been instrumental in persuading the others to keep the original team intact. In the course of the conversation, Ken mentioned that he intended storing the York at York Factory for the following winter. In the summer of 1996, he explained, the same crew, including me, would take the boat back upriver to Norway House. The idea certainly appealed to my sense of history.

Ken informed me that the departure for 1995 would now be in early July. Charlie, he explained, was committed to his job as a fishing guide until the end of June. I reshuffled my schedule to accommodate the latest change in plans.

To avoid one of the problems of the previous year, I ordered my own set of topographical maps from the land information division of Manitoba Natural Resources. With those in hand it was a simple job to calculate the distances between all obstructions from Oxford House to York Factory. At the same time I requested a set covering the first phase of the expedition.

I printed the details of all rapids beyond Oxford House and mailed the breakdown of the route to Ken McKay. As far as I could see we would have twenty-one sets of rapids to negotiate before the final 145 kilometres to York Factory. Many of the rapids sit close together, separated by no more than a few kilometres. The first rapid, a small one, is less than eight kilometres from Oxford House.

In late June the expedition was delayed again, until the end of the first week in August. Low water levels over the rapids were cited as the reason. It seemed like a strange excuse to me. As the summer progressed the water levels were more likely to go down than up. With the annual "York Boat Days" festival[4] due to take place in Norway House early in August, I had other doubts about the latest schedule. I couldn't imagine Ken and the crew leaving home prior to one of the highlights of their year. As a precaution I phoned him to check. He confirmed that the date had been changed yet again; this time to August 15. I was thankful I had taken the precaution of keeping my summer clear for the expedition.

I flew in to Winnipeg on August 12 and phoned Ken to announce my arrival and check on the latest plans. I had expected to fly to Norway House to join the crew immediately. Ken suggested I fly straight to Oxford House and meet them there as they would be flying in on two charter aircraft with limited room. With two days to spare, I remained in Winnipeg and visited friends until it was time to leave.

The weather, which had been so warm and friendly in Winnipeg, turned against us. It was raining lightly and very windy in Thompson when I changed planes. There was actually some doubt as to whether we would even be able to take off because the winds were so strong. One of the joys of flying with Canadian bush pilots is that they rarely let bad weather stop them. Even so, their safety record is second to none. Once airborne, the pilot announced we would have to fly to God's Narrows first, and then fly by line of sight to Oxford House as the beacon there was out of action.

Line of sight, under those conditions, sounded rather optimistic because the clouds were almost on the deck. We flew under the clouds, anyway. Later, the pilot told me we had flown the last eleven minutes at an altitude of five hundred feet above the ground. I thought we were much lower as the treetops appeared within arm's reach. Overhead, the clouds skimmed over the cabin roof, being parted momentarily by the knife-edged tail fin. We banked over Oxford Lake — there probably wasn't enough room over the trees — and made a low-level approach to a perfect soft landing.

Oxford House airport had not changed in a year. The same clapboard terminal building offered its dubious greeting. It looked as dowdy as ever in the gloomy conditions. Rain had been falling steadily all morning and the ground around the apron was muddy. I stowed my gear out of the way under a bench inside the building. More than two hours remained until the York boat crew came in. There was nowhere I wanted to go and nothing to do. I settled down with a book to wait for my fellow adventurers.

Weather conditions were far from perfect, but a succession of flights landed and took off safely. A short while before the charter flights were due to arrive, while I was outside checking the weather for the umpteenth time, Ben Paul ambled round the corner of the building. He had heard on the local radio that the York boat expedition team was coming in that afternoon. He seemed surprised to see me. Taciturn as ever, he said little.

We waited together, mostly in silence, until nearly 3:30 p.m., with no sign of the expected planes. Then, without a word to me, Ben suddenly walked back toward the settlement. He didn't come back. I continued to wait. I asked the air-traffic controller if he had any word of the flights. He checked with Cross Lake air-traffic control who said they were delayed due to bad weather. I waited some more. Later we were informed, after we initiated a call, that the flights had been cancelled due to bad weather and would be rescheduled for the following afternoon.

Oxford House is a smaller settlement than Norway House, with less than half the population. In 1995 it did not boast a motel, or any other form of commercial hostelry. I had visions of sleeping at the airstrip in my pup tent, or in the nearby forest. The York boat was beyond my reach across the river. I felt I should stay as close to the airstrip as possible, just in case plans changed again. In view of the inclement weather, Tim Muskego, the air-traffic controller, arranged for me to rent an apartment at the nurses' building for one night. Assuming it was to be my last opportunity to sleep in a real bed for a few weeks, I willingly paid the sixty-dollar charge. Neil Bradburn, another airport worker, then kindly drove me to the Northern store, at the other end of town, for a few basic food supplies. He waited while I shopped: there was more he wanted me to see. Not far from the store, he turned down a steep grassy track to the lake and showed me where the York boat had been pulled out of the water the previous summer.

I looked out at the lake. About fifty or sixty metres away, the York boat floated among the reeds where Oxford Lake bleeds into Back Lake. From a distance, it looked exactly as it had when I first saw it at Norway House, over a year before, except that it desperately needed a coat of paint. I asked Neil how much work was done on the boat when it was hauled out in the spring.

"Oh, I don't think they did much work on it," was his surprising answer.

Equipped for temporary survival, I walked back to my overnight apartment with dinner, breakfast, and lunch in a plastic bag. En route I mulled over the possibility that the York had not been properly repaired — or worse, had not been repaired at all. The thought of endless bailing didn't thrill me one bit. I vowed to insist the boat was hauled out for a close inspection of the keel and hull before departure. If there was anything wrong with the boat we would fix it in Oxford House.

There was no telephone at the residence and no working pay phone anywhere in Oxford House that I could find, except at the airport and that was closed by then. I was unable to tell anyone of my whereabouts, though I did not find this particularly concerning. I spent a quiet evening studying topographical maps and preparing myself for the following day when, I expected, we would be back on the Hayes River, or at least — on the York boat.

Oxford House came into existence as a white settlement in 1798. There are said to be remnants of the original HBC buildings within, or close to, the town site, but no one could tell me where. By the time the first group of Selkirk settlers arrived en route to the Red River in 1812, Oxford House was a small but thriving village, with its own vegetable gardens and some cattle.[5] Just over one hundred years later, in 1914, the Oxford Lake Cree signed a treaty that established a reserve around the old HBC post. As a result, Oxford House has grown into a substantial community of some 2,300 residents and an area of 12,000 acres (4,858 hectares).[6]

In the morning I arranged to leave my bags at the residence until midday and returned on foot to the airport. Tim told me the flights were due in by midday. I went for a long walk on the muddy winter road. From there I would hear, even if I couldn't see, any airborne arrivals. The weather had improved considerably, but the eagerly anticipated flights did not come in at midday. A few other flights came and went. Nothing came in from Cross Lake.

As the afternoon marched on, I phoned the charter airline company at Cross Lake myself. I was told they were still waiting for the Norway House passengers to arrive. No one there had any idea why the crew were not already at Cross Lake with their equipment. On an impulse I phoned Ken's home in Norway House and asked to speak to him. To my complete surprise I learned that Ken had gone to Winnipeg the day before, and the rest of the crew were still in Norway House. The expedition, I was told, had been cancelled, but no one had taken the trouble to send a message to me.

I told Neil of the cancellation of the expedition. He wasn't surprised. There were a few people in the airport building at the time. One of them said, "Those Norway House guys wouldn't make it anyway, the water's too low."

I argued in their defence. We had dragged the boat over beaver dams, run her down rapids, and portaged her through a burned-out forest. Given the opportunity, we could and would take her the rest of the way. I was really frustrated and feeling extremely let down, but there was nothing I could do about it. The simple fact was, the crew were not coming in: the boat would not be continuing its long journey to York Factory as planned. I had no alternative but to chalk it up to experience and, perhaps, another small anecdote to add to the history of the Hayes River.

Back to Winnipeg I went. As we took off from Oxford House I could see Back Lake behind the settlement, and the first set of rapids on the Hayes. Seconds later the York boat was below and to our right as we turned on course for Winnipeg.

At the end of August I had a long telephone conversation with Charlie. During that talk I told him, as I had done the year before on the shores of Oxford Lake, that I would be prepared to help repair the boat — if he could persuade the crew to continue the voyage, and I would go with them all the way to the bay. Unfortunately, despite our enthusiasm for the adventure, it was not to be. The York boat stayed where it was near Oxford House and the crew stayed home.

I had expected to get my first look at York Factory from the bow of a York boat surrounded by excited Cree tripmen. Instead, six years later than originally planned, I would get there by similar, but by smaller means.

CHAPTER 15
Three Canoes on the Hayes

OVER THE NEXT FEW YEARS I considered various ways of completing my journey down the Hayes River. For a time, unable to convince friends and acquaintances to go with me, either through their lack of time or interest, I thought of going alone. In fact, in 1997 I went as far as planning to go solo in the summer of 1999 or 2000. Whether alone, or with like-minded people, I estimated a minimum two-week run by canoe from Oxford House to Hudson Bay. For safety, considering food reserves and a definite pick-up time by air at the end of the river, I extended that to a maximum of three weeks. Then, while my fledgling plans developed, a message from a business associate in Winnipeg told me of a local expedition company preparing to paddle from Oxford House to York Factory by canoe in August of 2000. It was the answer to my dilemma. I immediately applied to join and was accepted. My on-again, off-again Hayes River voyage was on — again.

Six of us flew into Oxford House from Winnipeg on a warm, dry summer day. The airstrip building still looked the same. In mid-afternoon a local pickup truck hauled us, our equipment, and our three canoes to the launching site at the south end of Back Lake. Rob Currie and Mark Loewen, both biologists, are licensed canoe/ river guides. They are partners with their mentor, Bruno Rosenberg, in Wilderness Spirit Adventures, based in Winnipeg. In company with three others: two more biologists, Val and Herbert, and Barbara (another writer), we will run the 380 kilometres from Oxford House to York Factory together, come rain or shine, fair winds or foul.

We paired up, two for each canoe, agreeing we would change partners occasionally as the days progressed. For the first day Rob and Val took the lead canoe, Mark and Herbert the second, while Barb and I shared the third. Barb asked to take the stern seat and steer, with me in the bow. It worked reasonably well on the open expanse of Back Lake and at first on the river, until we reached the beginning of the rapids and swifts, where we discovered Barb was not strong enough to steer effectively. As we coasted toward the first obstacles on Kawapiskachowasik, she lost control and I, way out of practice, did not correct the canoe's drift in time. Within seconds we were turned broadside to the flow and trapped by the current against a rock. Mark waded back upstream and pushed us off, but, out of sync as we were, the river took charge again. We drifted backwards downstream a few metres until I could get the canoe turned and pointing safely in the right direction again. Mark suggested we reverse our paddling positions immediately. I moved to the stern and Barb took her place in the bow. Working together at last, we made it through the next couple of sets without incident or further embarrassment.

On the left bank, Rob's sharp eyes picked out a small black bear peering out of the bushes as we paddled past. A few minutes later we met two other canoes heading upriver. They were en route from Shamattawa, on God's River, to Oxford House. After that, we were on our own. Peace descended on the river. The only sounds were occasional splashes from our paddles and undertones of conversation coming from the three canoes.

We successfully navigated two more rapids, one with a virtually unpronounceable name due to the number of syllables in Kawepinikateekopasow, and the somewhat easier Kiasokanowak, before hauling out for the evening just above the long and difficult stretch of Knife Rapids. We secured the canoes to bushes on a granite ledge close to the river. A few paces inland we found a pleasant glade, just large enough for three tents and a cooking space. Carpeted in a thick layer of moss, the natural site offered a comfortable haven for our first night's camp.

With the camp set up and dinner over, Rob and I sat on rocks within sight of Knife Rapids, our feet suspended just over the river, and talked about our dogs. I'd had mine put to sleep only a few weeks before due to an inoperable brain tumour. She had been with me for nearly fifteen years and her loss weighed heavily on me. Rob missed his dog, too, but knew he would be reunited with him in Winnipeg at the end of our river journey. Later, with hands cupped around steaming mugs of tea, our conversation veered into literature.

Rob was reading something about India, a country he admitted he longed to visit. I was on the final chapter of Gabriel Garcia Marquez's *Love in the Time of Cholera*. In view of Rob's interest, I told him about my adventures travelling overland to India in the 1960s and 1970s. As we talked, we discovered our tastes in travel literature are similar. We agreed Robert Byron's *The Road to Oxiana* is probably one of the finest travel books ever written. I was well aware that many of Byron's lines, though written decades before, and about lands far away and considerably warmer, echoed my feelings for parts of my journey on the Hayes River. That evening, our conversation exhausted, we sat in silence for a while, watching the reflections of the moon and stars on the water passing by. It was, for me, as Byron wrote of the arrival of dusk during a visit to Shiraz while travelling through Persia: "One of those rare moments of absolute peace, when the body is loose, the mind asks no questions, and the world is a triumph …"[1]

Knife Rapids, aptly named for the sharp rocks that litter the lower levels, covers roughly two-and-a-half kilometres — where the river somersaults over and around boulders and islands. From our campsite, only a few metres west of the first drop, we could clearly hear the noise of rushing water on rocks at all times, no matter how loud our conversations.

In the morning we practised ferrying upriver and across the current until Rob was completely satisfied that none of us would become a liability on the nearby rapids. This time Barb travelled with Rob while Val took the bow seat in my canoe. Having all passed Rob's test, we set off one canoe at a time to follow a drop-and-eddy route, zig-zagging across the river as necessary to select the safest course. It was an exhilarating ride, yet, as I studied our approach to each set of rapids, I felt tension within me; not just with our downstream route, but also due to a sense of mystery as to how the nineteenth-century Cree tripmen managed to get their York boats safely up these same cataracts.

There was no way a heavy boat could be rowed up the rapids. The flow was much too strong for that. Equally, handlining in many places would have been a challenge due to the dense bush along the banks, which would have been just as thick during the fur-trade era: another natural barrier to progress upstream.

Once clear of the knife-edged rocks, the river led us quickly to the somewhat-easier-to-navigate Wapatakosanik Rapids. With those two trials behind us we pulled in to the east bank, just before a notorious, though quite magnificent waterfall, and hauled the canoes out of the water. Our confidence was high, but not high enough for a foolhardy attempt on Trout Falls.

Where the current rushes to get down to the next level, the river is sharply divided by large rocks in mid-stream and drops suddenly about four to five metres. Running the falls was never an option for us. As with the York boat and canoe brigades of the HBC era, we followed a short, traditional portage route to get around the falls to the safety of a large eddy quite close to the foot. A confusion of bare tree trunks lay scattered over the rocks at the eastern end of the portage. Close inspection showed that they had been placed there by human hands as a ramp to enable a boat, or boats, to be more easily moved from one level to the next. The effect was similar to that which we had employed for the York boat on Robinson Portage in 1994.

When the Franklin expedition came through here in September 1819, Midshipman Hood took the time to sketch Trout Falls. In addition to a remarkably accurate rendition of the scene as we later saw it, Hood added a dozen or so men hauling a York boat up the portage we descended 181 years later. Franklin commented: "…The beauty of the scenery afforded a subject for Mr. Hood's pencil … The rocks which form the bed of this river are slaty [*sic*], and present sharp fragments, by which the feet of the boatmen are much lacerated."[2]

Trout Falls, where portaging is the only option. The tree lengths at bottom left show where a basic track had been used to portage boats from the upper level to the lower.

We were fortunate that we did not have to labour in the water in bare feet. From Trout Falls we again changed partners, Herbert taking up bow position in my canoe. As we pushed away from the rocks and sped downstream toward Knee Lake, the weather worsened. The overcast sky lowered and soon the river was pocked with rain. We donned our waterproof ponchos and, with heads bowed against the downpour, kept on paddling. Just before entering the lake, a strong current, rather akin to the outer edge of a whirlpool, swept us close to steep, smooth granite on the south shore. We paddled harder to free our canoes from its grip and escaped to the open waters of the lake.

High winds added their force to the rain. They hit us head-on as we began the long, exposed slog down the shin of Knee Lake. Just pushing foward was a daunting task. Pelting rain and an unpleasant chop of over half a metre, with occasional big waves, added to the difficulty. Instead of camping and waiting for an improvement in the conditions, which could take days, we elected to keep going. For a few unpleasant hours we forced our canoes onward, the carrot of Knee Lake Lodge[3] and the possibility of a hot shower keeping us going. Travelling side by side, though with each canoe separated from the others by twenty or thirty metres, we traded shouted thoughts, occasional curses, and a lot of off-colour jokes.

During a lull in the chat, as we pushed hard against a series of powerful gusts of wind, I tried to imagine myself back on a torpid jungle river in the humid warmth of Bangladesh. My imagination was not equal to the task that day. Try though I might, I couldn't come up with any suitable sweaty thoughts, and failed to generate any appreciable warmth in my mind or body. I gave up the attempt at fantasy and concentrated on the task at hand. Dig deep with my paddle and drive the blade back. Dig deep. Drive back. Dig deep. Drive back. *Allons! Allons! Allons! We must go on.* Beaudelaire back in my mind again. The repetition good for me and the rhythm I needed to maintain. Dig deep. Dig deep. Dig deep.

Despite our hardships, nothing nature threw at us that day could completely dampen the enthusiasm or humour of the six canoeists. As we progressed down the lake, the jokes continued, though less often than earlier in the day. Someone asked Rob what he thought about while he was paddling for hours. Without hesitation, he yelled back, "Sex!" Everyone laughed and dug their paddles in with renewed energy, all, perhaps, thinking the same thing.

Each stroke of the paddle reacted against increasingly sore muscles. My right arm and shoulder began to hurt more than I could handle. To gain some relief I paddled only on one side of the canoe, instead of switching from side to side every so often. Herbert was in the bow of my canoe and had no choice but to paddle only on the opposite side for over an hour to balance my strokes. I felt sorry for him, but he was gracious enough not to complain when we finally stopped for the day. When I told Rob about the problem later, he looked at me in mock horror and said, "I would have killed you."

By the time we pulled up to a dock near the lodge in the late afternoon, Barb, the smallest and thinnest of us, was shivering uncontrollably. We wrapped her in a sleeping bag and hustled her into the warm as soon as we could before looking after ourselves. We were all soaked through, cold, tired, and hungry. That evening we each had a hot shower, dried our wet clothes, and dined happily on excellent lodge fare in the staff kitchen. With appetites satisfied and bodies clean again for a while, we put up our tents on a grass lawn near the boat dock and slept easily. Not even the lodge's noisy generator could disturb my sleep that night.

At daybreak the rain had gone, the clouds dispersed, but a strong wind persisted from out of the northeast. There was little chance of making any significant headway in canoes. Late in the morning Rob negotiated a lift for us and our canoes to the end of the lake in two motorboats. A couple of hours later, under clear skies and a hot sun, we were dropped off on a narrow beach at the far end of the lake, where it funnels into Cebanakasipee Bay. Rob guessed we had just saved two days of hard paddling into the wind.

I had wanted to stop and take a look at Magnetite Island, situated close to the bend, or knee of the lake at Opishikona Narrows, about one-quarter of the way along from west to east. A small prominence, no more than forty metres across, the islet contains magnetic iron ore that has an extremely unsettling effect on compass needles. Franklin noted that his compass was affected for a distance of some three hundred yards from the source on both the approach and the departure. He commented that, on the northwest side of the islet, the needle on one compass "dipped so much that the card could not be made to traverse by any adjustment of the hand …"[4]

Despite my wish to spend a few minutes experiencing the magnetic phenomenon for myself, the high winds and our unplanned motorboat ride put paid to the idea. We sped past and all I could do was look back with a certain degree of disappointment.

Where the lake and bay turn into a relatively narrow waterway again, the river takes on a strong current and soon the rapids begin once more. We camped for a night on the east bank of the river at Paktikonika Rapids. No more than fifty metres away, a pair of bald eagles sat and watched us from the vantage of their substantial nest high in the fork of a tree. Paktikonika is classed as CIII–CIV.[5] Consequently, to successfully challenge its power requires more than basic canoeing skills. Many canoe expeditions take the easy portage route instead of risking the rapids. We all wanted to test ourselves so, leaving the canoes at the camp, we walked the length of Paktikonika on the portage route to study the various aspects of the run. Old moose droppings and fresh bear scat littered one narrow part of the trail through the undergrowth, causing a few raised eyebrows. After crossing a narrow log bridge we reached the second and third drops. Not as extravagant as the initial falls, they still posed their own potential for upset.

Once we had seen the full extent of the problems we faced, and with good visibility, meaning no hint of rain, we all agreed we could handle it. While I fished for northern pike in reeds above the rapids, and for walleye immediately below the first set to restock our supplies, the others made practice runs in empty canoes down the first part of the torrent.

Mark and Herbert made a spectacular run at high speed while Val and I watched from the bank. Rob and Barb followed a minute or two later, the bow of their canoe reaching high as it hit the first standing wave. Once they were safely down, Rob put Barb ashore and Val took her place. Together they went back to keep watch on Mark and Herbert, who were practising their combined skills in the turmoil at the foot of the first cataract. With Val in the bow, Rob cruised about in his canoe some distance downstream, prepared to effect a rescue in case of an upset. It was a wise precaution. When the inevitable happened, Mark's canoe suddenly flipped, throwing both he and Herbert into the whitewater, Rob was alongside in

© Anthony Dalton Collection.

Rob Currie and Valerie Hodge getting wet on Paktikonika Rapids.

seconds, guiding the upturned canoe and its paddlers to safety. On the bank we cheered all three of them: two for their bravado, and one for his highly skilled rescue response.[6]

My turn on Paktikonika came the following morning. With all three canoes hauled back to the upper level, we loaded them and tied everything down. Once out in the stream there was no turning back. At one with the current and increasing speed to maintain steering control, we raced over the drop in line astern — each canoe separated from the next by two or three lengths. We shipped some water and skidded momentarily; then we were through and racing for the second and third set, fully charged with adrenaline. Without slowing our pace, we hurtled past blurred rocks on both sides and reached for the next challenge. It was not far away.

After Paktikonika the rapids kept us busy all the way to the beginning of Swampy Lake, as much with the fun of running them as with the difficulty in pronouncing their Cree names: a couple of choice ones on this section being Apakisthemosi and Apithapakiticanona. The former is rated as CII to CIII and the latter a CII,[7] both obvious rock gardens with strong potential for bumping and grinding by missing the best lines. Val and Herbert worked together on the run down this stretch of rapids, while Mark took the bow spot with me. Without actually rolling or sinking our canoe, Mark and I got soaking wet, challenging each drop with as much speed and energy as we could muster. Mark's exuberance got us close to trouble a few times while his superb paddling skills kept us on track and safe. Val and Herbert enjoyed themselves, too, although they did get hung up on rocks a couple of times, but soon fought clear. Barb and Rob, in the third canoe, ran all drops with precision and without apparent effort. I think we had more fun.

The weather closed in on us again as we completed that stretch of rapids and came out onto the western end of the lake. The wind stayed away, but heavy rain haunted us all the way from one end to the other. In the early evening, after a miserably hard day of paddling, we camped on a small island covered in trees. We were soaked and cold again and, as usual, we were hungry. Desperately hoping the rain would stop in the night, we hung our wet clothes on lines strung between trees. They could not get any wetter anyway. With the "laundry" taken care of, Mark and Rob mixed up scalding hot chocolate to warm our insides while we cooked dinner. We were lucky. The rain did stop around midnight and some of the clothes were almost dry by morning. With the wind blowing hard directly upriver, we spent the morning getting the rest of our clothes dry, exploring the beautiful little island and waiting for calmer weather.

We had already suffered more than our share of rain and high winds. After each downpour and each hard blow, we prayed for good weather to carry us to the bay. The weather continued to be unpredictable. Fortunately, when the rain stopped during the day, the huge Manitoban skies welcomed us and saturated our tired muscles with life-giving heat from a benevolent summer sun.

CHAPTER 16
Rapid Descent

AFTER CLOSE TO A WEEK back on the river, my ears were once again attuned to its sounds, especially the dull roar of whitewater cascading over rocks. At one rapid, unnamed as far as we knew, we stopped our three canoes and huddled together in an eddy, out of the main stream. A light rain drizzled on us as we discussed the upper slopes of the long descent the tripmen of old called Hill River. Those intrepid men had their own names for each of the rapids and knew exactly how many paces were involved in portaging round them. Of the fourteen drops on the long and potentially dangerous incline between the top of Hill River and the Rock, tripmen noted that the portages varied in length from a casual forty paces to a strenuous walk of five hundred paces.[1] Lightly laden compared to the HBC boats, we planned to avoid portaging and handlining where we could by running as many of the rapids as possible.

The ever-present thunder of yet another big rapid caused us to raise our voices as we considered our options. In the previous few days I had shared a canoe with each member of the expedition. On that day I was again partnering Mark: the youngest and the oldest working as a team. He stood in the stern of our canoe, supporting himself by moving his paddle lazily in the slowly moving eddy and studied the nearby rapids. A light rain fell, adding to the mist where the water boiled. I knew what Mark was thinking: it was written on his smile. We could do it.

Rob, standing in an adjacent canoe, looked doubtful. He resumed a sitting position and recommended we try the left channel. Mark continued to stand, his paddle barely moving; our canoe almost stationary. He looked at me in the bow. The expression on his face told it all. He wanted to run that rapid and, as I was his paddling partner, I got to vote, too. It was hard to ignore the wistful boyish grin. I looked over at Rob, who shrugged his shoulders and smiled. He too knew exactly what Mark wanted to do.

"All right, Mark. Let's do it." I'm sure there was a note of resignation in my voice. I knew it would be a rough ride — a wet ride. I tightened the chin-strap on my crash helmet and dipped my blade in the water. Back in the nineteenth century, during each summer this part of the river echoed with the shouts of tripmen racing down rapids or handlining uphill against the extreme current and constant natural obstacles. The shouts on that August day would come from me and from Mark.

Watched by our companions, we dug our paddles deep, urging the long red canoe upstream about fifty metres, so we could set the line we wanted to follow for our planned route over the first and largest drop. At Mark's brusque command we ferried left and turned through 180 degrees. We were then one with the current, yet we had to go faster.

From shore a canoe racing toward rapids gives the impression of immense speed. On board, moving marginally faster than the current, our descent began as if we were in slow motion. I could see the line we must take. I could see the lip of the drop, where snarling water washed smooth boulders and jagged rocks clean. It was shrouded in mist and approached almost leisurely until … I disappeared into the miasma, leaving Mark no choice but to follow. The current changed our pattern of travel: it was no longer in slow motion. At full speed the canoe leapt over the rocks nose first into a permanent standing wave of icy history. Instinctively I shouted, "Oh, ---!" The expletive out before my lips were sealed by an avalanche of river pouring into my face and over my head, flooding the canoe. I dug my paddle deep, helping Mark keep us straight, too busy to be scared. We broke through, skidding right then left, over another smaller drop, searching for calmer water. Without floatation bags fore and aft, we would have sunk for sure. Loaded to the gunwales with our equipment and a full cargo of river, we took the safest route, ferrying right, across part of the main current, to the calm of an eddy behind a convenient rock. Mark punched the air with his horizontal paddle and yelled his jubilation to the world. I was happy, too, apart from the fact that we were soaked right through, again.

The other two canoes chose an easier line and made it through in a less dramatic fashion. They waited for us on the other side of

© Anthony Dalton Collection.

Herbert Koepp and Mark Loewen taking a wet and wild ride down the hill.

the river as we bailed all the water out before ferrying back across to join them.

There are forty-five sets of rapids of varying sizes and severity from start to finish on the Hayes. Most of these are on the second half. The longest section, which we had just started to descend, is a nonstop watery stairway past Brassey Hill,[2] at 392 feet (120 metres) above sea level — the second-highest point in Manitoba. Rapid follows rapid in quick succession and most of them need to be scouted from shore. Some are too dangerous to attempt. Without exception, their names evoke the strong ties this river has with the Cree nation — more unpronounceable names such as Neesootakuskaywin and Apetowikossan. Few have names we could understand, let alone twist our tongues around the complex syllables. Many of the rapids tested our skills. Rob and Mark made their decisions on which ones to run and which ones to avoid, based on our levels of competence. They were the experts. We willingly followed their lead. With each rapid safely run our abilities improved and our confidence increased accordingly.

About halfway down, and ready for a break after tackling a long series of drops culminating in High Hill Rapids and followed by a long stretch of fast ripples, we pulled in to shore at the foot of Brassey Hill and secured the canoes. The river at this point is lined on the east side with a tight weave of willow bushes. Access to the land is restricted to a few places. An animal trail, littered with scat and just wide enough for one person at a time, meanders through the foliage a few metres from the river. Bent on climbing Brassey Hill, for the view as well as much-needed exercise for our legs, we crossed the trail and pushed upwards.

The highest point between Lake Winnipeg and Hudson Bay, the tree-covered hill is a strenuous climb. With no defined route to follow, we worked our way up through the forest, clambering over fallen tree trunks and pushing through thick undergrowth at times. The view from the top over the surrounding lakes is said to be quite spectacular. For us, no such view was possible. Low clouds enshrouded the summit and rain began to fall. No one seemed to mind. We had all enjoyed the ramble through the woods. We made our descent, more at a trot than a walk, in half the time it had taken for the climb. By the time we reached the canoes, the rain was driving down in force. Resisting the temptation to stop where we were protected to some extent by the umbrella of trees, we agreed to suffer. Poncho time on the river again.

Once back to work, and paddling into the cold rain of a series of line squalls, I kept thinking about the early fur traders and the journeys they made each season up and down this magnificent river. How did their journeys differ from ours? The answer was not difficult to find. They each had to expend enormous amounts of energy for weeks at a time, especially on the uphill slog, in all kinds of weather conditions. No matter how hard we found the paddling at times, we were on a vacation cruise in comparison. We could, within reason, stop whenever we chose to wait for good weather. We were in control of our own destinies. Later, standing on rocks overlooking yet another dangerous chute, I couldn't help but wonder at the extreme effort needed to manoeuvre those heavy freight canoes and even heavier York boats back up this determined river. Especially on the wild and painful uphill stretch where rapid follows rapid for so many kilometres.

Robert Ballantyne expressed the difficulties well, even though he was travelling in a relatively small canoe: "Our troubles now commenced: the longest and most difficult part of the route lay before us, and we prepared for a day of toil. [As] far as the eye could reach, the river was white with boiling rapids and foaming cascades … we were obliged to make portages at almost every two or three hundred yards."[3]

Ballantyne later refers to one of his "Indian" companions guiding their boat through "a chaos of boiling water."[4] The Cree, with whom Ballantyne forced his way up the Hill River, employed a stepping-stone route: paddling hard against the current from one rock to the next by resting in the eddy at the downriver face of each one. He likened their progress to that of a salmon fighting its way upstream to the spawning grounds. When paddling against the powerful current proved impossible, the Cree used long poles to keep their canoes on track and moving forward.[5]

Overhead, bald eagles entertained us by performing aerial ballets, and occasionally an osprey rocketed out of the sky to snatch an unsuspecting fish from the middle of the channel. Taking a tea break from paddling into torrential rain on a narrow strip of beach, we found fresh wolf tracks. Some days later, once we had raced beyond reach of the rapids, Rob would find us another black bear, a cub this time, running away from the approaching canoes in panic.

Descending the rapids, whenever possible, we camped each night on smooth rocks with the roar of the next day's adrenaline rush in our ears. Each night I attempted to supplement our larder with fresh Northern pike. Voracious eaters, prepared to take anything that looks remotely edible, they are not hard to catch. Most nights, and often for breakfast, for those who enjoy it, we had pike: occasionally a choice of pike or walleye.

When the rapids were too rough even for Mark's enthusiasm, we either portaged or carefully lowered our fragile craft down the safest route by the use of handlines. We followed on land, scrambling over rocks and through bushes to keep the canoes from getting away from us. Inevitably, prior to Brassey Hill, on the first cascade of Kakwa Rapids, one broke free and sped away with the river. Within seconds it had diminished in size to no more than a red speck in the distance. While the rest of us waited back on shore, Mark and Rob raced in pursuit in another canoe. Fifteen minutes later they came back with the errant vessel in tow. Although we handlined our canoes at Kakwa, we could have followed a really obvious traditional portage trail over a long, wide, flat rock. It was a perfect roadway for the York boats of history.

On one stretch, where the river widens and thunders over a ledge, it also separates along one side into an extremely shallow channel to pass around an island. Well aware we could not risk the main falls, we chose the side channel instead. For most of the ten or so minutes it took to make the detour, we could feel the bottom of our canoes bumping on stones and our paddles dug into the riverbed instead of clear water. Twice I had to step out of my canoe and float it free of obstructions. The advantage of the detour was that we re-entered the main river a short distance downstream from the falls. Looking back, we could immediately see why Rob and Mark had taken us on the shallow, but infinitely safer route.

Secure in an eddy a little upstream from another wide and raucous rapid, holding on to shore-bound bushes to keep still, we watched and listened as the river crashed over the multitude of rocks. There was no way we could run this one. We could not handline from the side we were on, and there was no portage route. Rob pointed to the opposite side of the river where a series of low, flat rocks projected from the bank. He spoke quietly to Barb and headed back upstream, ferrying the two of them expertly across the main flow to the opposite bank without obvious concern. A few minutes later, standing on rocks beside the rapids, he motioned with his arms, telling us to join him. Well aware that I was the oldest member of the group, Mark leaned over and asked me if I was comfortable with making the crossing. I nodded, my face set and my eyes on the river. Without another word, Mark and Herbert followed the ferrying route taken by Rob and Barb, their combined power getting them upstream and out of danger in a matter of minutes. Our turn. For a few seconds, perhaps close to a minute, I sat still — staring at the river rushing past — willing the adrenaline to build in my body. In the bow, Val turned to look at me, waiting for my signal. Across the turbulence, standing on the safety of the opposite bank, Rob, Barb, and Herbert stood still, their eyes on us. Rob looked worried. Mark sat in his canoe, close by them, also watching us, his paddle moving slowly and easily to maintain his position in the eddy. A bald eagle flew low overhead, whistling its strident call. It sounded like a command to me. I answered immediately.

"Let's go, Val."

As one we dug our paddles in deep and powered upstream until we were close to the lower end of an earlier rapid. Off to my left I could see Mark maintaining his station parallel to us, but close to the bank out of the main stream. Choosing my position carefully and working with the current, we, too, ferried safely across to calmer water. There, clear of the tumbling and spray, we slipped along the bank from eddy to eddy, with Mark — one of our two resident whitewater rescue experts — slightly downstream from us, but never far away. At the rocky maw of the rapid where the others waited, we nosed in to shore. Barb greeted me with her gamine grin and a lively, "Man, you are a tough old bastard."

I followed Val ashore, stopping only to accept her delighted high-five. Rob grinned at me from under his crash helmet and nodded his satisfaction. I felt as though I had just passed some kind of endurance test.

With all of us together again, we carefully handlined the three loaded canoes one after the other down the rapid into a quiet bay beside a sloping rock. Ahead we could see many more rocks and whitewater spray. Mark and Barb led the way, followed by me and Val. Rob and Herbert took their position a few canoe lengths behind us. Carefully, we wove the canoes through the hazards at each drop and down safely to the next level.

It had been a tough day. The constant progression of rapids, with the need for vigilance and constant hard paddling, had worn us all down, but we were almost at the end. Just ahead, around a few more corners, was Whitemud Falls, the final big rapid, known as "the Rock"[6] to the tripmen of old.

The current, which had not slackened a whit since we began our descent of Hill River, increased. We knew we must keep tight

© Anthony Dalton Collection.

Herbert Koepp and Mark Loewen running Whitemud Falls, the last major rapid on the Hayes River.

to the left bank in order to get ashore on one of the rocky islands overlooking the main rapid. Any other course would put us at the mercy of the main flow before we could scout a safe route. Paddling carefully, it only took a few minutes for us to pass the first main island and power across a few metres of turbulence to the next, slightly larger flat rock. About two-thirds of it is covered in small willows, but there was enough room for three canoes, three tents, and space to dry our clothes and relax. Barb, tough though she is, visibly dragged her feet as she helped set up a tent. Her slow movements reflected the way my muscles felt.

The HBC's William Tomison built Rock House Depot near here in 1794.[7] Rock House had dwellings for the factor and staff, warehouses, and, it is said, a large vegetable garden. The fishing was good, too. Rambling across the shore on the north side of the rock there's a big patch of bulrushes; they suggested pike to me. A little farther out, where an eddy begins, there was an opportunity for walleye. Tired though I was, the thought of fresh fish was impossible to resist. Within far less than an hour of casting I had lost a couple of lures in the bulrushes. To compensate, I had three good-size pike and one walleye ready for cleaning and eating. Dinner doesn't get any fresher than that. We spent the final few hours of daylight writing our journals, tidying equipment, and, for me at least, watching the river. Whitemud Falls fascinated me. It looked deadly, but I knew from history, with the right skills, it could be run in safety. Today it is classed as a CIII,[8] but it looks and sounds much worse when standing at its edge.

The next morning we planned to run the big chute — because we could and because we had to. It was the last big drop on the river. Our egos would not allow us to portage round it, although the portage would be quick and easy to handle. It was a case of do or die. The thought flashed across my mind and I'm glad my mouth didn't repeat it. We did not need any bad omens at this stage of the river. As we broke camp and loaded the canoes, I found myself looking

Barb Scot and Rob Currie taking a perfect line at Whitemud Falls.

up every few seconds and watching the unchanging pattern of the river powering down over the final big drop to the Hudson Bay Lowlands: just as I had done the evening before. I'm sure the others also offered the falls their own furtive looks.

When the moment for departure came, one canoe at a time, we paddled back upstream, pushing ourselves hard, until we could round a small islet and safely get into the main flow. From that point there is only one way to go and that is down. I had wanted to run that particular rapid since I was a boy in England and first read Ballantyne's account of his adventures with the Hudson's Bay Company. He wrote of coming in sight of these rapids from the northeast while on his final journey up the Hayes in late June 1845:

> As we approached the cataract, a boat suddenly appeared on the top of it, and shot at the speed of lightning into the boiling water beneath, its reckless crew shouting, pulling, laughing, and hallooing … In this manner seven boats successively ran the fall…[9]

One hundred and fifty-five years after Ballantyne's experience, it was my turn (though in the opposite direction) and I took it with my heart pounding. Once out in the strong main current and facing downstream, I was committed. Trying to get back to one of the islands of flat rock was not an option. It was time to go. The banks flashed by and the spray flew up ahead of us. The run was over before I knew it. I must have picked the right line because, although I got myself and my partner very wet, we didn't hit anything solid and skidded safely out of the mainstream into calmer water on the right bank. I don't remember clearly, but I'm sure I pumped the air with my fist in exhilaration. I had made it. Another dream realized. *We* had made it as a team. The hardest and, perhaps, the most exciting parts of the river were behind us, but we still had a long way to go and a lot more to see.

The "Rock," the end of which can be seen at lower left, signals the end of the major rapids on the Hayes River.

A convoy of HBC boats working hard to make their way upriver to Rock Fort in September 1821.

CHAPTER 17
Final Days on the Mighty River

AFTER WHITEMUD FALLS THE RIVER takes a permanent break from its mad rush down off the Canadian Shield. That was the last of the rapids, although there were a few swifts ahead. The oddly named Berwick Falls proved to be nothing more than a long series of riffles over a bed of stones, instead of the noticeable drop some of us had anticipated. Berwick was also named Borthwick or Borrowick,[1] the name varying from book to book and document to document. The river is shallow and fast, streaming over loose stones and rocks: too shallow for York boats and the heavier freight canoes. For the tripmen, this equated to a portage of forty paces[2] to get boats past the worst section. We were able to keep to the river and, although we did a little bumping and grinding, we did not have to step out of our canoes.

After Berwick Falls we could let the current do all the work. It was fast enough, about nine or ten kilometres per hour, to carry us long distances each day. We had a deadline to meet, however. A chartered plane was due to pick us up opposite York Factory one week later. In view of that fact, we would have to assist the current by paddling each day in case we were held up by headwinds coming in from the bay.

When we stopped for lunch on a comfortable grassy bank, being hungry, my mind turned to fish as usual. Around two hundred metres or so upstream, a creek meandered off to the northwest. It looked to be a near perfect spot to find a few tasty brook trout. I was about to paddle back upriver and try a few casts when the distant chatter of a helicopter diverted my attention. A few minutes later, the noisy machine flew low over us, circled past a bald eagle trying to get out of the way, and came back for a gentle landing close to our canoes. On board was an independent television production crew working on a documentary of the Hayes River.[3] With them as an advisor was Rob and Mark's partner, Bruno Rosenberg. While the TV crew interviewed first me then Barb about our stories, Bruno handed over three bottles of single-malt Scotch and a selection of English and Irish beers to Rob and Mark for future use: medicinal purposes only.

Barb, a former high school teacher, mountain climber, and naturalist living in Portland, Oregon, is the author of three nonfiction books. Her latest at the time, *The Stations of Still Creek*, is a haunting model of beautiful writing. Barb's reasons for being on the river, like mine, included research for a book. As part of that study program, she had already visited Kildonan in Scotland, and Churchill — on the shores of Hudson Bay. From the latter point she travelled by snowmobile along the inhospitable Hudson Bay coast at the tail end of winter, with a Native guide, to York Factory. With her on the Hayes, as a tangible reminder of her project, she carried an antique pewter goblet: the Cup of Kildonan. At the conclusion of our expedition at York Factory she planned to go home and write her story from an historical perspective, but based on personal experience.

The helicopter's departure an hour later for a convenient filming spot a short distance downstream signalled the time for us to

© Anthony Dalton Collection.

The canoe team take it easy and drift down the lower reaches of the Hayes River.

get moving, too. We needed to cover a lot of miles before nightfall. That fact didn't stop us from being lazy. After an energetic start for the benefit of the cameras, we relaxed as soon as we were out of sight and took advantage of the sun and the fast current for a while. Holding the three canoes together, we lay back and floated for a few hours under a scorching sun, only bothering to paddle when a bend in the river threatened to put us ashore. The steep clay banks, lined along the top with motley collections of healthy and some broken trees, trap the sun within their walls and attempt to control the river's current. The river, imperturbable, carves its own passage as it follows its destiny. One of the early settlers bound upriver for a new life likened the clay banks to the White Cliffs of Dover.

R.M. Ballantyne came up the Hayes River the first time by York boat in September 1841.[4] At that time, this section of the Hayes was known as the Steel River. Ballantyne noted that the current was too strong for the boat to be rowed, so men had

Steep clay banks line the Hayes River as it courses through the Hudson Bay Lowlands. One traveller commented that they reminded him of the White Cliffs of Dover.

to be sent ashore to track the boat upriver. With lines run out, half the crew went ashore to struggle with the boat and the terrain, while their companions slept on board for an hour. They then changed over so that each crewman worked for an hour then rested for an hour. Those rest periods were highly necessary. Sometime the men on shore trotted along at river level. At others they had to scramble up the often unstable cliffs and work from narrow ledges; sometimes from the top of the cliffs among the trees. It was back-breaking and time-consuming work. Even so, according to Ballantyne, the crew he was with stayed cheerful and made the journey from York Factory to the Rock at Whitemud Falls in just five days.

Two years later, Ballantyne made the return journey to York Factory, commenting that the only event worth reporting on the downriver run was when his canoe struck a rock and had a hole torn in its side.[5] He did not discuss the length of time he took to travel from Norway House to the bay. In 1845, when Ballantyne made his final journey on the Hayes River, again travelling upstream, he was in a light canoe with two Cree. Despite being detained by strong winds on some lakes, the small party took twelve days — covering an average of fifty-four kilometres each day — to get from York Factory to Norway House. Not a fast run, but impressive to us latter-day voyageurs, anyway.[6]

At the confluence of the Hayes River and Fox River we camped on hard earth opposite Wachichakapasew, the Crane's Breast Cliff. It was at this important river junction that Pierre Radisson first made contact with the Swampy Cree in 1685:[7] a meeting that would eventually have great significance for the future Hudson's Bay Company. Radisson returned to his ship, moored in Ten Shilling Creek — on the east side of the river not far upstream from the York Factory site — with a valuable cargo of furs.

There were no Cree at the junction when we arrived and no wildlife visible, although once again wolf tracks crossed our chosen campsite. While the others set up camp, Mark and I paddled upstream a little on the Fox River to go ashore at the base of the cliff. It is steeply pitched and about twenty metres in height. From the rocky shore I studied the clay wall, hoping to see a climbable route to the top. There are obvious handholds and footholds, but they crumbled at my touch. Climbing to the top for the view, which had been my plan, had to be abandoned in the interests of safety: the risk of breaking a limb in a fall was too obvious. Vaguely disappointed, I returned to the canoe and we paddled speedily back to camp to help prepare dinner.

Later, standing beside the Hayes and looking up the Fox River, I wondered about that route. Why didn't the tripmen use it? Studying the appropriate topographical maps to find out showed the Fox to be a much smaller river than the Hayes, but with at least as many, if not more, rapids and falls. The Hayes, its difficulties notwithstanding, was the better route to the interior.

From my journal:

> Day 10. Sat in a natural pool in the river and had an all-over wash after a lousy night's sleep. Fresh wolf tracks on shore this morning, again, and throughout the camp. Considering I was uncomfortable and awake most of the night, I'm surprised I did not hear them. Saw a black bear cub on the west bank soon after we started this a.m. The weather has been weird. For a while today it looked as though we would have a major storm, but only a few raindrops fell. We decided the ominous sky was the result of a distant forest fire. We drifted again for a couple of hours rafted together. There's no sense of urgency today. Only 7 kms from God's River tonight. About 97 kms to York Factory.

Just before noon on our eleventh day on the Hayes, we joined God's River. It begins its journey across the lowlands at God's Lake, only about twenty miles southeast of Knee Lake. Once God's River appears, with two busy flows combined, the Hayes widens even more and the current keeps it moving fast. Islands grow in midstream. The main banks drift farther apart. After intermittent rain in the morning, the afternoon welcomed us with a downpour to equal an Asian monsoon. We donned our ponchos and kept going. It was far from pleasant out in the open canoes, but no one wanted to stop and make camp early. We passed a few apparently abandoned cabins, but there was no suggestion of stopping for shelter. The rain poured off our ponchos and sweat ran down our bodies under our clothes. We couldn't have got much wetter. With heads bowed against the rain, we paddled stroke after stroke for what seemed like an eternity until Rob angled toward the east shore and called a halt. We had some time in hand and he had decided that continuing out on the river in such conditions was pointless, as well as most uncomfortable. Soaked through, we could not agree more.

For the next twenty-four hours, we endured torrential rain. We stayed put. There was nothing to do, but doing nothing was infinitely more appealing than paddling in that weather. Throughout the daylight hours we congregated in the cook tent, drinking tea, coffee, or hot chocolate, occasionally laced with excellent Scotch, and telling off-colour jokes, all the while standing in ankle-deep mud. No one complained. Occasionally one of us would wander away to the tents to sleep for a while, or to read, or just relax. In the afternoon, with no let-up in the weather, I went for a walk in the rain, hoping to surprise or be surprised by a wild creature. I was disappointed, but the exercise was beneficial to my legs. And I felt better just doing something physical.

The rain eased off in late evening, just in time for the clouds to break and the setting sun to colour the eastern trees with crimson fire. It was spectacular. Satisfied with nature's efforts to brighten our lives, we slept soundly and awoke to a beautiful day. No one was in a hurry so we dawdled over breakfast and in loading the canoes. Once on the river, we rafted together for an hour and drifted on our backs with the current. Above us, the clouds created an ever-changing gallery of surrealistic art: dolphins, a narwhal, a swordfish, a white horse, and a parasol trailing a long, silken tail. Then there was a ghost, a giant tadpole, a turtle, and a couple of whales. I could have drifted and slept for hours but, someone was awake.

"Time to work," Rob announced as he sat up and pushed his canoe away from the others. Minutes later we were all driving our canoes hard, determined not to be left behind. With paddles flashing and spray flying we saluted the Pennycutaway River as we passed in the early afternoon and knew that York Factory was only a day away — the end of our journey though history. Pennycutaway is a corruption of the Cree name *Punagutweo* — meaning "Light the

Fire River."[8] I posed the question of why the river was given such an enigmatic name, but no one could tell me.

We spent our final night on the river on the north shore of Four Mile Island. A beach of sand and small pebbles, backed by long grass and high, untidy willow bushes, offered plenty of room for our tents and canoes. We stripped off and took a swim in the cold, clear water, cleansing our bodies of nearly two weeks of hard effort and revelling in our successful expedition. I wandered off alone for a long walk, finding the expected recent wolf tracks and a few interesting-looking stones. That night the heavens staged a spectacular display of thunder and lightning to celebrate our arrival. For hours the thunder rippled across the sky from one horizon to the other, sounding like a nonstop high speed tattoo on a snare drum. We stood together in the cook tent out of the rain, drinking hot chocolate, telling jokes as usual, and watching the storm's fierce beauty.

The morning dawned clear and warm. As we collapsed and folded the tents, an Osprey took a fish right in front of us, close to our canoes, while Mark and Herbert were swimming naked in the river a few metres away. Our warning about the potential for a grievous personal loss if the osprey came back was greeted by hoots of laughter. Rob and I had our canoe loaded first and, eager to reach York Factory, we sped away from the final camp. Mark, standing in his birthday suit in knee-deep water, immediately launched himself at us in a racing dive. For a few seconds we thought he might catch us and tip us over but, with four arms and two paddles to work with, combined with a strong survival instinct, we pulled ahead. Out in the stream and clear of Mark's mischievous intent, we relaxed and let the current do the work until the other two canoes caught up.

As we drifted, Rob regaled me with a couple of his inexhaustible supply of jokes, but I wasn't really listening. I was at peace. With nothing strenuous to occupy me, I ignored Rob, closed my eyes and let my mind drift back to Homer and a line from *The Odyssey*: "Smooth flows the gentle stream with wanton pride ..."[9]

The river was smooth and, on that day, I was a little sad. We were close to the end of the exciting and potentially dangerous Hayes River. We had challenged its might and we had won. Relaxing after its headlong rush over scores of rapids, it settles into a benign state, running smoothly almost in sight of the bay. Inevitably, I thought of Ken McKay and his Norway House crew with some nostalgia and wondered what they were doing at that moment. With my eyes closed, I could almost see the York boat: her red sail raised and filled with wind, Ken on the steering sweep, eight rowers led by Charlie slamming their oar blades into the river in unison to add an additional touch of speed and romance. Distantly I could hear an old echo, "Aha, boys! Oho, boys! Come on, boys! Let's go, boys!" Instinctively I obeyed, digging my paddle deep and pulled back. Our canoe surged forward as I tried to keep pace with the mental image. Rob's voice, greeting our companions as they joined us, brought me back to reality: to the present. There was no York boat there — just three canoes spread out across the river and six happy paddlers. An hour after leaving Four Mile Island we tied up to the jetty at York Factory. We were all smiling.

One by one we climbed the rickety wooden staircase up the cliff. At the top, on a field of green grass with the stark white façade of the one large surviving York Factory building in the background, we stood beside a sign welcoming us to the site. There we shook one anothers' blistered hands and offered congratulations all round for our achievement.

CHAPTER 18
York Factory

Y ORK FACTORY, ONCE A SIZEABLE HBC fur-trading settlement with
many wooden houses, was closed down in 1957 and is now a
National Historic Site of Canada administered by Parks Canada. The
one significant remaining original structure is "The oldest and largest wooden building in Canada standing on … permafrost."[1] In its
"glory" days of the mid-nineteenth century, especially in summer,
York Factory was a hive of activity. Although the number of permanent residents hovered around forty men, on occasions there were
far more people there. Ships arrived from England with eager settlers
bound for the distant interior while fur traders came in from the
opposite direction. Brigades of York boats and freight canoes travelled the hundreds of miles of rapids on the Hayes River, between
distant interior settlements and York Factory, carrying bales of furs
downriver to the sea and an eclectic variety of cargoes on the much
more strenuous return journey. Immigrants, fur traders, and tripmen
congregating for a few days turned York Factory into a busy fort.

The first known white man to visit this area was a British naval
officer named Sir Thomas Button. With two ships, Button and

his crews sailed from England in May 1612 on a voyage in search of a route from Hudson Bay into the elusive Northwest Passage. After safely navigating through the difficult tides and drifting ice of Hudson Strait, Button sailed to the mouth of the Nelson River. The two ships spent the winter there, during which the larger vessel, *Resolution*, was crushed by ice. As the ice retreated in the spring of 1613, Button followed the coast north in the pinnace *Discovery*, reaching an eventual high latitude of sixty-five degrees. Unable to find the route he sought, Button returned to England.[2]

Seventy years later Pierre Esprit Radisson, a Frenchman who never seemed to be sure whether he wanted to work for French or English masters, established a small trading fort on the Nelson and explored the Hayes River estuary. The original York fort was built by the Hudson's Bay Company in 1684 on traditional Cree hunting ground. The French, who had their own fur-trade agenda, captured the fort a decade later. They held it for two years until the British took it back by force. Not to be outdone, the French recaptured York Factory in 1697 and named it Fort Bourbon.[3] The remote fort continued in French hands until the signing of the Treaty of Utrecht in 1713. That significant document awarded exclusive trading rights on Hudson Bay to the Hudson's Bay Company. The French packed their bags and left Fort Bourbon soon after, and the British, in the guise of the Hudson's Bay Company, reclaimed it as York Factory. The present-day site of York Factory is actually the third location used for the fort by the HBC. The original site, in use from 1684 to 1715, and the subsequent site — which lasted somewhat longer, from 1715 to 1788 — were located a short distance downstream. The factor at the time, Joseph Colen,[4] chose the current piece of high land after spring flooding caused problems in 1788. After the departure of the French, the HBC stayed for the next 244 years. The Cree stayed with them for most of that time.

It is interesting to note that the British had two enormously powerful companies operating in far distant lands at the same time.

The Hudson's Bay Company, which began life as the Company of Adventurers in 1668, controlled a substantial area in North America during the eighteenth and nineteenth centuries, and lasted well into the twentieth century, at much the same time the formidable Honourable East India Company dominated the Indian sub-continent for close to three hundred years.

With the Hudson's Bay Company firmly back in control of its eponymous bay, York Factory gradually grew in size to a major trading post, which in turn expanded until it became the HBC's headquarters for its fledgling Northern Department in 1810. Not only was York Factory the administrative centre for the company's far-flung spider's web of remote trading posts, it was also the transportation and transshipment hub for inbound and outbound goods.[5] In the first half of the 1800s it was, in addition, most often the first contact with land in North America for untold numbers of European immigrants heading for the prairies and farther west. The ordeal of their transatlantic crossings, followed by the dangers of Hudson Bay, were only precursors for what was ahead on the wild rivers for those naive yet brave new arrivals.

Due to the late arrival of three ships from Scotland, the York Factory area was obliged to play host to over one hundred men, the first group of Selkirk settlers, over the winter of 1811–1812. The men had sailed from Stornoway in the Hebrides in late July in the HBC ships *Prince of Wales*, *Eddystone*, and *Edward and Ann* and only arrived at Five Fathom Hole on September 24, too late to attempt the Hayes River with winter about to set in.[6] With not enough space to accommodate such a large party at the post, the new arrivals sailed the short distance to the Nelson River and spent an icy winter on its banks in houses they built from logs and clay. With the advent of spring and ice break-up, those who still wanted to, or who were still able, could finally continue up the Hayes in early July 1812. They reached their ultimate destination, where the Assiniboine and Red rivers meet, in what

Hudson's Bay Company Archives/Archives of Manitoba/HBCA P-158.

Sailing of the Hudson's Bay Company ships *Prince Albert* and *Prince Rupert* from Gravesend, England, on June 8, 1845. Most HBC ships departing for Hudson Bay ports left from Gravesend, including *Nonsuch* — the first of many.

is now downtown Winnipeg, at the end of August. Many more were to follow.

As mentioned earlier, Lieutenant John Franklin came through York Factory in 1819 on his inland expedition to the Arctic. He was only one of many explorers to visit York Factory.

In the early summer of 1841, a flotilla of three sturdy sailing ships — *Prince Rupert*, *Prince Albert*, and *Prince of Wales* — waited at anchor in the busy Thames estuary off Gravesend for the signal to depart. All three were owned by the Hudson's Bay Company and all three were bound for Hudson Bay ports. *Prince of Wales* had orders for Moose Factory on the southern tip of James Bay, while the other two were destined for the mouth of the Hayes River. They were large sailing ships for the time, each one being well in excess of one hundred feet (thirty metres) in length and displacing roughly four hundred tons (362 metric tonnes). All three were rigged as barques. *Prince Rupert*, the sixth such HBC ship with that name in honour of the company's founder, carried a teenage Scottish boy among its passengers. Robert Michael Ballantyne, who I have quoted a few times in this book, was fifteen years old when he left Britain and his family to work as a clerk for the HBC. Ballantyne described his first impressions as *Prince Rupert* arrived at the anchorage for big ships at Five Fathom Hole:

> Here, then, for the first time I beheld the shores of Hudson Bay; and truly their appearance was anything but prepossessing. Though only at the distance of two miles, so low and flat was the land, that it appeared ten miles off, and scarcely a tree was to be seen. We could just see the tops of one or two houses in York Factory, the principal depôt of the country, which was seven miles up the river ...[7]

Ballantyne later described the settlement which he would get to know well during the next few years (although he changed the distance from the river's mouth):

> The fort ... is a large square, I should think about six or seven acres, enclosed within high stockades, and planted on the banks of the Hayes River, nearly five miles from its mouth. The houses are all of wood, and, of course, have no pretension to architectural beauty; but their clean white appearance and regularity have a pleasing effect on the eye.[8]

Ballantyne spent two years at York Factory before making his first journey up the Hayes River. He wrote of those informative months with relish, obviously having enjoyed the experiences as only a young man of the times with an enquiring mind could. He also, rather rudely, referred to York Factory as "a monstrous blot on a swampy spot, with a partial view of the frozen sea."[9]

The various buildings of York Factory were connected by wooden walkways (footpaths). Office Street looking north.

Only twenty-two years before Ballantyne, in August 1819, Midshipman Robert Hood had not been at all impressed by his first sight of York Factory, or of its personnel, although he was not, perhaps, as critical as Ballantyne would later be:

> It consists of several wooden buildings inclosed [*sic*] by stockades or wooden spikes four or five yards in length, driven into the ground. The principal building is two stories high, with a courtyard in the interior ... The whole has the appearance of a temporary erection by shipwrecked seamen, and the resemblance may be carried further in the occupations and varied garbs of the inhabitants, who seemed to be clothed in what they had snatched by chance from destruction."[10]

In September 1845, while ascending the Winnipeg River in a large birchbark freight canoe with two European companions and eight muscular paddlers, Ballantyne encountered the famed Dr. John Rae travelling by canoe in the opposite direction. Typical of a man with his wilderness skills, Rae was alone and en route from Sault Ste. Marie to the Red River Settlement. From there he and a small party sailed the length of Lake Winnipeg to Norway House in a York boat and continued down the Hayes River to York Factory. Rae happily spent the winter at York Factory before sailing north for the Arctic. I was only there for twenty-four hours, but I, too, would have liked to stay longer. Time, however, was not on my side.

I stood beside a Parks Canada sign welcoming visitors to York Factory. Behind the sign across the neatly trimmed lawn stood a pair of modern houses; home to the resident rangers in summer. They represent the present. My mind, however, was on history. I looked northeast beyond the distant river mouth toward Five Fathom Hole, hoping perhaps to see the impossible: a large, wooden sailing ship ghosting in to the anchorage. Five Fathom Hole was empty, of course, as was the estuary — just as they have been throughout each

Library and Archives Canada/PA-041571.

York Factory from the air in 1925, with a two-masted sailing ship at the jetty.

summer since the post was shut down in 1957. Despite the lack of ships, history is alive in this remote part of Manitoba and nowhere is it more apparent than in the depot.

A factory, in the sense of the HBC posts, is defined as, "a station where resident factors trade." York Factory, one of the earliest, was originally laid out in the shape of a large H, with the depot building, the guest house, and a summer mess house combining to form the centre bar facing the river — its highway to the riches of the hinterland and to the nearby sea. Storage houses for furs, plus provision shops, trading rooms, officers' and servants' quarters made up the parallel lines enclosing the centre bar. The depot, or "Great House," which the Cree called Kichewaskahikun, was the undoubted focal point. All other buildings, such as the church and clergyman's residence, the doctor's house, smithy, bakery, cooperage, various dwellings, and the powder magazine, among others, were built in a less formal arrangement and connected by a series of boardwalks.

Only two buildings remain today of the more than fifty which once occupied the extensive site. The main, or depot, building is now a museum of Hudson's Bay Company activities on the Hayes River and on Hudson Bay, both of which can be clearly seen from upstairs windows. Within the depot's walls can be found archival photographs, stained-glass windows in their original frames, a cast-iron stove, an array of cannon, and numerous other archaeological artifacts from the fur-trade era.

While studying the old black-and-white photographs on the walls, I stopped in front of a faded image of a sailing ship standing at anchor in the river in front of York Factory. She rested there, with all sails furled, guarded by a cannon sited on the grounds in front of the depot. The brief caption told me her name was *Ocean Nymph*[11] and that the photograph dated back to 1880. Built in Quebec City in 1862, she sailed from ports on the St. Lawrence River to York Factory and other Hudson Bay posts on behalf on the HBC, as well as making several crossings of the North Atlantic.

Geological Survey of Canada/Library and Archives Canada/PA-039914.

The HBC ship *Ocean Nymph* at anchor in the Hayes River under the shadow of York Factory's cannon (1880).

For a time, in 1866 and 1867, she even took part in the Company's abortive whaling enterprise centred around Marble Island in the northwestern extremity of the bay.

The list of ships that called at York Factory during its 273 years of history is long. Apart from a series of ships named *Prince Rupert* (there were at least six bearing that name over the course of two centuries), a trio of the more noteworthy vessels included *Discovery*, which served from 1905 to 1912. She was a three-masted, barque-rigged auxiliary steamer built of oak in Dundee, Scotland, in 1901. Her main claim to fame is that she carried the ill-fated British naval officer, Robert Falcon Scott, on his first Antarctic expedition between 1901 and 1904. She now resides in graceful silence on the north side of the Thames River in the heart of London, England.

Discovery was preceded by another three-master: the two–decked auxiliary steamer *Erik*. She, too, was built at Dundee, though for the Greenland whale fishery. After entering the HBC's service in March

1887, she was dispatched across the North Atlantic to Labrador. In 1892 she became the first Company steamer to enter Hudson Bay.

Built for the British Admiralty in 1877, *Pelican*, a composite[12] screw sloop later strengthened for use in ice, joined the HBC fleet in 1901 as a replacement for *Erik*, which had recently been sold to a Scottish businessman. She supplied York Factory and other posts on Hudson Bay and into the eastern Arctic until 1916.

There was, for a time in the early 1900s, an HBC schooner named *York Factory*, which carried cargo along the west coast of Hudson Bay between York Factory and posts distant as Coats Island in the north opposite the western end of Hudson Strait.

The waters of Hudson Bay have exacted a harsh toll on shipping since the seventeenth century. York Factory being on the southwest coast of the bay meant that ships had to run the ice and fog gauntlet of Hudson Strait, followed immediately by a complete crossing of the notoriously stormy bay. Consequently, many of the vessels

An HBC ship, passengers, and crew in the ice of Hudson Bay.

owned by or chartered by the HBC suffered severe damage or were lost. In September 1836 the hermaphrodite brig *Esquimaux* arrived at York Factory with a damaged rudder. A few weeks later, while en route up the coast to Churchill, she ran aground and had to be abandoned. Also in 1836, the brigantine *Eagle* went up on the rocks off Button Island and spent the winter in the Hayes River near York Factory. In September 1859, *Kitty* was wrecked in Hudson Strait. One of the lucky HBC ships was aptly named *Perseverence*. A three-masted barque, she made one voyage from London to York Factory and Churchill in 1891. From June 1892 to October 1897 she spent the summers on whaling voyages in Hudson Bay and Strait, without getting into any noteworthy trouble. After two years in British waters, she returned to Hudson Bay in the summer of 1900 on a voyage to Moose Factory at the foot of James Bay before being sold in 1901.

With my fellow paddlers, I took a stroll along the boardwalk (strategically placed wooden planks) to avoid ploughing our feet through wet mud, to the nearby cemetery set in a grove of slim trees. Aware that polar bears are known to roam the area, we kept watch on all sides and kept our conversations above normal levels. The cemetery contains 161 identifiable graves from the late fur-trade era and after, the latest of which — the final resting place of Albert Arthur Saunders — has a marker engraved in the Cree language.

In 1997, as I worked on ways to continue the long journey downriver from Oxford House to York Factory, I had some extended correspondence with Councillor Eric Saunders of the York Factory Cree First Nation. As a result, Eric sent me much useful information on his people and on York Factory as it is today and as it was. Although I did not get to meet Eric (he was home in York Landing, far inland on the east bank of the Nelson River, about halfway between the bay and Lake Winnipeg), the day we arrived at York Factory we had coffee with Jim and Betty Settee of Parks Canada. Later that day, as we moved our three canoes downstream a short distance to the Silver Goose Lodge, we met two more Cree, Howard and Jim, with their husky, Sheba. Standing on the old HBC site, six years after my original journey started in Norway House, I felt that I had come full circle. My two-part expedition across a large tract of Manitoba commenced with members of the Cree First Nation and it has been completed by visiting a handful of Cree at a traditional First Nations' homeland close to the mouth of the Hayes River.

Rob's shotgun has the York Factory symbol, a combined Y and F, burned into its stock. That brand was put there by Jim Settee on a previous visit to York Factory. It is identical to the brand burned or stamped onto bales of furs, packing cases, and sundry other packages by the HBC to mark their passage through York Factory and, therefore, their ownership. At my request, Jim graciously heated up his iron and burned the brand into a block of wood for me as a souvenir of York Factory.

Although we don't know the name of the first factor to take up residence on the Hayes River at York Factory, we do know that a George Geyer was its first HBC governor.[13] He was in charge from 1686 to 1690. Not much is known about him, other than that he was a contemporary of the explorer Henry Kelsey, who was employed at York Factory at the same time. The last factor to serve the Hudson's Bay Company at York Factory was Albert Bethune "Toots" McIvor.[14] Born at Cross Lake in 1899, McIvor joined the HBC as a young man, following in his father's footsteps. His first job was that of store clerk and interpreter, before working his way up to take full charge of the post. After his retirement he wrote of his final days at York Factory: "It [York Factory] was in operation for 275 [sic] years and I have often wondered whether I should have felt honoured for being the last Post Manager or ashamed for being the one who closed it."

Polar bears are often seen roaming the site during the summer, as they probably have done forever, and beluga whales frequent the Hayes estuary, as do a variety of species of seals. Although

Glenbow Museum Archives/NA-1041-7.

A sailing ship in the Hayes River estuary and a two-masted York boat at York Factory's jetty.

we kept alert, and rather hoped we would encounter one as our canoes approached York Factory, we saw nothing moving on land to suggest the presence of a white bear. The river was also almost empty to our view. No whales blowing in the estuary, just a solitary harbour seal raising its head near the jetty to look at our canoes as we arrived.

On our last night on the Hayes we sat together on the roof of one of the cabins at Silver Goose Lodge and sipped our Scotch while watching the final rays of sunlight playing on the clouds. There was the threat of a thunderstorm that failed to materialize. The following morning, while waiting for our chartered plane to come in to the airstrip on Hay Island across the estuary, I stood alone on the grassy lawn in front of the great white building that is now all that is left of York Factory. Instinctively, I looked down at the river and northeast toward Hudson Bay. The adventurer in me began to stir: I wondered what it would be like to run before the wind on a sailboat out there and explore the islands and coastlines stretching to the north? Far, far to the north — where the Arctic winds blow strong and hard. Indeed, I wondered.

For the moment, though, the personal odyssey that started for me six years before at Norway House had finally reached its conclusion. I had reached my goal and I was content. The treasure I sought in the adventure of this journey was mine.

> If the treasures to which we had the key
> The plan the map and the lovely adventure
> Should only prove a dream and an imposture
> Think of them still ... think of them still ...[15]

The end.

Notes

Epigraph

1. This enigmatic quote from an unknown author was also used by Pierre Berton to open his epic 1972 tale, *Klondike, The Last Great Gold Rush 1896–1899.*

Preface

1. The Second World War aerodrome, or airfield, which the author explored as a boy in England, was the former RAF Mount Farm, situated just west of Dorchester, Oxon, and about thirteen kilometres (eight miles) southeast of Oxford. The flooded gravel quarry was close by.

2. On and around Mount Farm in the late 1940s and early 1950s, the author studied a variety of birds native to that part of Britain, plus voles and rabbits, and during one summer caught a few harmless grass snakes, plus one poisonous adder.

3.   The author and his wife lived in Antwerp from early 1993 to mid 1997.

CHAPTER 1: ROWING DOWN THE RIVER

1.   The chant is based on the last word of the fifth verse of Charles Baudelaire's *Le Voyage,* which he wrote for nineteenth-century French writer and photographer Maxime du Camp.
2.   The quotation is the tenth verse of Charles Baudelaire's *Le Voyage.*
3.   Baudelaire's stepfather (Jacques Aupick) sent him to sea in June 1841 in an attempt to divert him from the questionable company he kept in Paris. Baudelaire would later draw on those nautical experiences, and his forays into the ports en route, for many of his longer poems.
4.   This quotation is from the first verse of Rabindranath Tagore's song, "Pilgrim of Life." The English translation of the full verse reads "Pilgrim of life, follow thou this pathway: Follow thou the path which the afternoon sun has trod, ending the day."
5.   "The Hudson's Bay Company ... came into being in its earliest form in 1667 in London, England." Glyndwr Williams, "The Hudson's Bay Company 1670–1920" *The Beaver* Special Issue (Autumn 1983): 4.
6.   "The first Stock Book of the Company ... records that in 1667, some three years before the granting of the Charter [The Royal Charter granted by King Charles II to 'The Governor and Company of Adventurers of England trading into Hudson's Bay'], substantial sums of money had been provided for the enterprise." Sir William Schooling, *The Hudson's Bay Company 1670–1920* (London: The Hudson's Bay Company, 1920), 4.

7. Prince Rupert of the Rhine, one of the founders of the Company of Adventurers, and the first governor of the HBC, was a tall (six feet, four inches) and valiant military strategist, sailor, scientist, inventor, politician, and entrepreneur. He was also said to be a superb tennis player. Born in Prague in late 1619 of mixed but royal European blood (he was the grandson of King James I of England), he went to England in 1642 to fight for King Charles I in the Civil War. He was thereafter a fixture at the Royal Court until his death in November 1682. Charles Spencer, *Prince Rupert, The Last Cavalier* (London: Weidenfeld and Nicholson, 2007).

8. Based on reports from two French adventurers (Radisson and Groseilliers), Prince Rupert was able to convince King Charles II to lend his support for a fur-trading expedition to Hudson Bay.

9. *Nonsuch* details: From a memorandum dated May 17, 1966, held in the HBC Archives, Winnipeg.

10. Zachariah Gillam (1636–1682) was born in Boston, Massachusetts, to a prominent New England family. A sailor and contemporary of Radisson and Groseilliers, he captained *Nonsuch* on its first and only voyage for the Company of Adventurers. Gillam died at sea when his ship, HBC's *Prince Rupert*, dragged its anchor and foundered in a storm off the north shore of the Nelson River estuary. Source: *Dictionary of Canadian Biography Online* (www.biographi.ca/009004-119.01-e.php?&id_nbr=308&interval=25&&PHPSESSID=3et2q132b9nb2q9avc15e3ipc7, accessed June 2009).

11. Médard Chouart, Sieur des Groseilliers, often referred to as Mr. Gooseberries by the English, was an explorer and fur trader. Born at Charly-sur-Marne, France, in July 1618, he and his trading partner (also brother-in-law), Pierre-Esprit Radisson were instrumental in the foundation of the Company of Adventurers, which became the Hudson's Bay Company.

12. King Charles II ruled England, Scotland, and Ireland from 1661 until his death in 1685. He signed the Royal Charter which gave Prince Rupert and his syndicate the right to trade:

> ... in all those seas, straits, bays, rivers, lakes, creeks, and sounds, in whatsoever latitude they shall be, that lie within the straights commonly called Hudson's Straights, together with all the lands, countries and territories, upon the coasts and confines of the seas ... which are not now actually possessed by any of our subjects, or by the subjects of any other Christian Prince or state ... and that the said land...[shall be] called Rupert's Land ...

Source: Sir William Schooling, *The Hudson's Bay Company, 1670–1920*. (London: The Hudson's Bay Company, 1920), 5. The author's copy contains a certificate stating: "Presented by the Governor and Company of Adventurers of England Trading into Hudson's Bay, to Mr. P.G. Shallcross to commemorate the 250th Anniversary of the grant of the Royal Charter. 1670 — 2nd May — 1920." The certificate is numbered 0 467.

13. The quote from the *London Gazette* of October 11, 1669, was reported in an HBC document headed "The First 'Nonsuch'" datelined Beaver House, London, E.C., July 4, 1968. It is now held in the HBC Archives, Winnipeg.

14. York Factory, named in 1684, held a pre-eminent position as a trading post and an entrepôt within the HBC for over two centuries. With the advent of improved supply methods to the vast area known as Rupert's Land on the southern route (via the St. Lawrence River) in the latter part of the nineteenth century, York Factory's importance faded to that of a regional trading post and, eventually, in 1957, to closure. Source: Parks

Canada (www.pc.gc.ca/eng/lhn-nhs/mb/yorkfactory/index. asp, accessed October 2009).

15. Ballantyne agreed with the comments on mosquitoes. He wrote: "During part of summer the heat is extreme, and millions of flies, mosquitoes, etc., render the country unbearable. Fortunately, however, the cold soon extirpates them." Robert Michael Ballantyne, *Hudson Bay; or, Everyday Life in the Wilds of North America* (London: Thomas Nelson and Sons, 1901), 189.

16. Most of the Company's lower echelon employees were referred to as servants to distinguish them from the gentlemen. Glyndwr Williams, 53.

17. David Thompson arrived at Churchill in the autumn of 1784. He was alone, fourteen years old, and about to start his first job as an HBC clerk. In the next twenty-eight years he travelled some 55,000 miles across North America, exploring and surveying. He became a skilled cartographer and is credited with drawing many of the earliest accurate maps of Canada. David Thompson, *Travels in Western North America 1784–1812*, ed. Victor G. Hopwood (Toronto: Macmillan, 1971), 3.

18. Dr. John Rae, the HBC doctor, surveyed some 1,765 miles (2,840 kilometres) of previously uncharted territory, travelled in excess of 6,000 miles (9,600 kilometres) on snowshoes. He also sailed thousands of kilometres in small boats. He eventually determined the fate of Franklin's Northwest Passage expedition and discovered the final navigable link in that elusive passage. Ken McGoogan, *Fatal Passage: The Untold Story of John Rae, the Arctic Adventurer Who Discovered the Fate of Franklin* (Toronto: HarperFlamingo Canada, 2001).

19. At the age of approximately twenty-two (his birth date is un-known) in 1689, the HBC sent Henry Kelsey from Albany House to Churchill. From there he roamed north along the coast to trade with the "northern Indians." One year later he travelled west into Assiniboine country where he covered

large distances in his quest for furs. He is credited with being the first white man to explore the prairies of what is now Saskatchewan and Alberta. Harold A. Innis, *The Fur Trade in Canada*, Revised edition (Toronto: University of Toronto Press, 1956), 121–122. Kelsey eventually became Governor of York Factory. Peter C. Newman, *Company of Adventurers* (Toronto: Viking Penguin, 1985), 293.

20. On behalf of the HBC, in 1719 James Knight sailed the west coast of Hudson Bay searching unsuccessfully for a link to the Northwest Passage. Neither Knight nor his two vessels and crew ever returned. The remnants of the ill-fated expedition were found on Marble Island in 1767. Peter C. Newman, *Company of Adventurers*, 291–298.

21. In his colourful career with the HBC, Samuel Hearne visited most of the company's forts on James Bay and Hudson Bay. He was the governor of Prince of Wales Fort (Churchill) and suffered the ignominy of having to surrender it to French forces in 1782 due to being hopelessly outnumbered. He is best known for his impressive overland trek from Hudson Bay to the Arctic Ocean. Ken McGoogan. *Ancient Mariner: The Amazing Adventures of Samuel Hearne, the Sailor Who Walked to the Arctic Ocean* (Toronto: HarperFlamingo Canada, 2003).

22. Historian George J. Luste referred to Samuel Hearne as the "Marco Polo of the Barren lands" in his essay, "History, Travel, and Canoeing in the Barrens," published as a chapter in Bruce W. Hodgins and Margaret Hobbs, eds., *Nastawgan: The Canadian North by Canoe & Snowshoe* (Toronto: Dundurn Press, 1987).

23. From the CHRS website: www.chrs.ca/Rivers_e.htm.

24. *Ibid*.

25. George Simpson was appointed governor of the HBC's Northern Department in 1821. He travelled extensively and at speed throughout his appointed domain in his large freight canoe. Over the course of his stewardship he "moved swiftly

from place to place …, investigating, probing, recommending, and sometimes dismissing." Glyndwr Williams, "The Hudson's Bay Company and The Fur Trade: 1670-1870," *The Beaver*, Special Issue (Autumn 1983): 51–52.

26. HMCS *Chippawa* is not an actual ship. Commissioned in November 1941, it is a shore recruitment and training establishment (often referred to as a "stone frigate" by naval people) in Winnipeg, Manitoba.

27. The author owned an expedition company working in the Sahara, sub-Saharan West Africa, and, later, the Middle East during the 1970s. At this time he also made his first journeys into the Canadian Arctic.

28. Lake Winnipeg (area). Source: *Britannica Online Encyclopedia* (www.britannica.com/EBchecked/topic/645470/Lake-Winnipeg , accessed June 2009).

CHAPTER 2: THE HISTORIC HAYES

1. "The Hayes River …" from Graham Dodds, *The Hayes River, Canadian Heritage Rivers System (CHRS) Background Study*, (Ottawa: Parks Canada, 1987),1.

2. Manitoba Parks Branch (www.manitobaparks.com).

3. Parks Canada (www.pc.gc.ca/eng/rech-srch.aspx?kw=Hayes%20River).

4. Pierre-Esprit Radisson. Peter C. Newman. *Empire of the Bay* (Toronto: Madison Press, 1989), 31–34.

5. In 1667 Sir James Hayes owned £1,800 worth of stock in the new Company, more than twice as much as any other stock holder. Harold A. Innis, *The Fur Trade in Canada*, Revised Edition (Toronto: University of Toronto Press, 1956), 124.

6. The Pleistocene Era lasted from 1.8 million to 10,000 years before the present day.

7. The list of mammals possibly to be seen on or near the Hayes River is from: The Hayes River, Canadian Heritage Rivers System (CHRS) Background Study.

8. *Ibid.*

9. *Ibid.*

10. *Ibid.*

11. *Ibid.*

12. Robert Hood, *To the Arctic by Canoe, 1819–1821*, ed. C. Stuart Houston (Montreal and London: McGill-Queen's University Press, 1974), 33.

13. Sir John Franklin, *Journey to the Polar Sea* (Köln: Könemann, 1998), 52.

14. *Ibid.*

15. The sources are too many to quote, but most books about the fur-trade era on the Hayes River agree on the nomenclature of the different sections that make up the complete river. This information can be seen on the illustrated map, *The Middle Track & Hayes River Route,* a hand-drawn map by Réal Berard and published by the Manitoba Department of Natural Resources, Parks Branch.

16. R.M. Ballantyne. *Hudson Bay: or, Everyday Life in the Wilds of North America* (London: Thomas Nelson and Sons, 1901), first among a long list of adventure books from Ballantyne.

17. *Ibid.*, 201.

18. *Ibid.*

19. Graham Dodds, *The Hayes River, Canadian Heritage Rivers System (CHRS) Background Study*, 51

20. Heather Robertson, *Measuring Mother Earth, How Joe the Kid Became Tyrrell of the North* (Toronto: McClelland & Stewart, 2007), 176–177.

CHAPTER 3: NORWAY HOUSE

1. The Northern store evolved from its beginnings with the North West Company and later the HBC.
2. Raymond M. Beaumont. *Norway House: A Brief History* (Norway House, MB: Frontier School Division No. 48, 1989).
3. *Cree Syllabics Dictionary.* Author unknown. Photocopy of a typewritten dictionary, possibly unpublished. For additional information on Cree syllabics see www.omniglot.com/writing/cree.htm.
4. "There are 40 syllabic characters …" From the introduction to *Cree Syllabics Dictionary*, 1.
5. Raymond H. Beaumont, *Norway House: A Brief History*, 33–36.
6. Alan D. McMillan, *Native Peoples and Cultures of Canada*, 2nd ed. (Vancouver/Toronto: Douglas & McIntyre, 1995), 12.
7. Raymond H. Beaumont, *Norway House: A Brief History*, 35.
8. *Ibid.*, 36.
9. Alan D. McMillan, *Native Peoples and Cultures of Canada*, 111.
10. Raymond M. Beaumont, *Norway House: A Brief History*, 1.
11. *Prince of Wales* was an HBC ship of 351 registered tons (356 tonnes) and licensed to carry eighty passengers. She served on the Hudson Bay route from England for an incredible forty years (1793–1841) and for many of those years was a regular visitor to York Factory. Source: HBC Archives, ships' descriptions.
12. Raymond M. Beaumont, *Norway House: A Brief History*, 17.
13. Because it would keep for long periods without going bad, pemmican was a daily staple for York boat crews. It was made from animal fat, lean buffalo meat or beef, and dried blueberries or Saskatoon berries. It could be eaten in its natural state, cooked, or boiled and made into soup by the addition of flour and water. (Source: A Parks Canada leaflet headed "Recipes" and containing information [in English and

French] on making pemmican and bannock. Collected by the author at Lower Fort Garry, Manitoba, in 1994.)

14. Raymond M. Beaumont, *Norway House: A Brief History*, 19.

15. The amalgamation agreement between the North West Company and the Hudson's Bay Company was signed on March 26, 1821. Harold A. Innis, *The Fur Trade in Canada*, revised edition (Toronto: University of Toronto Press, 1956), 280.

16. Raymond M. Beaumont, *Norway House: A Brief History*, 22.

17. *Ibid.*, 32

18. Alan D. McMillan, *Native Peoples and Cultures of Canada*, 111.

19. Sweetgrass (*Hierochloe odorata*), also known as Holy Grass, is considered sacred by First Nations peoples (and Eurasians). One of four sacred plants (the others are cedar, sage, and tobacco) it is used in purification rituals. Once dried it is braided to preserve its scent. The three strands of the braid represent mind, body, and spirit. When burned slowly, the smoke of the smouldering sweetgrass rises and is thought to take prayers to the Creator (www.nativetech.org/plants/sweetgrass.html).

20. According to the Canadian Government Definitions of Indian Status, October 1999 report, "The 'Metis' represent the second constitutionally-recognized Aboriginal group under Section 35 of the *Constitution Act* [The first group includes: Status Indian, Non-Status Indian, and Bill C-31 Registered Indian]. The national body which is acknowledged as representing this community is known as the Metis National Council. According to the Metis National Registry, a 'Metis' person is defined as: 1) a person who self-identifies as a Metis; 2) a person of Aboriginal ancestry (i.e., at least one grandparent is or was Aboriginal); and, 3) a person who is not registered on the Indian or Inuit Register."

21. York Boat races have been held on Playgreen Lake at Norway House each August since 1973. Part of the Treaty and York Boat Days, the races are a test of stamina and skill. York boat

rowers come from across Manitoba and farther afield to take part. Source: Norway House Cree Nation.

22. Philip Goldring, *Papers on the Labour System of the Hudson's Bay Company, 1821–1900*, Volume II, Manuscript Report Number 412 (Ottawa: Parks Canada, 1980), 137.

23. *Ibid.*

24. *Ibid.*

25. *Ibid.*, 135.

26. *Ibid.*, 140.

27. *Ibid.*

28. Peter N. Peregrine and Melvin Ember, eds., *Encyclopedia of Prehistory, Vol. 2. Arctic and Subarctic* (New York: Springer, 2001).

29. Graham Dodds, *The Hayes River, Canadian Heritage Rivers System (CHRS) Background Study* (Ottawa: Parks Canada, 1987), 19.

30. The Manitoba Historical Society (www.mhs.mb.ca).

CHAPTER 4: YORK BOATS

1. Joseph Conrad, *The Mirror of the Sea,* new edition (Plainview, NY: The Marlborough Press, 1988), Chapter XXXVI, *Initiation*, first sentence.

2. Dennis F. Johnson, *York Boats of the Hudson's Bay Company* (Calgary: Fifth House, 2006), 11–12.

3. *Ibid.*, 13, 27.

4. Philip Goldring, *Papers on the Labour System of the Hudson's Bay Company, 1821–1900*, Volume II, Manuscript Report Number 412 (Ottawa: Parks Canada, 1980).

5. Rock Hill River was an alternate name for the lower section of the Hill River, the part of the Hayes that runs downhill past Brassey Hill.

6. Thole pins, made of wood or of metal, are set in pairs on the gunwales of rowing boats to keep oars in place.

7.   R.M. Ballantyne, *Hudson Bay; or Everyday Life in the Wilds of North America.* (London: Thomas Nelson & Sons, 1901), 104.

8.   R. Glover, "York Boats" *The Beaver* (March 1949): 22.

9.   Dorothy L. Boggiss described her experiences in a York boat in: "York Boat Coming!" *The Beaver* (June 1954): 50–51.

10. John A. Alwin. "Colony and Company, Sharing the York Mainline" *The Beaver* (Summer 1979): 4–11.

11. Mary Inkster wrote of her journey from Churchill to York Factory in a York boat for the Summer 1979 issue of *The Beaver* (page 49).

12. Dennis F. Johnson, *York Boats of the Hudson's Bay Company* (Calgary: Fifth House, 2006), 97.

13. *Ibid.*, 50.

14. Farley Mowat, *Tundra* (Toronto: McClelland & Stewart, 1973), 276–278.

15. Dennis F. Johnson, *York Boats of the Hudson's Bay Company*, 61.

16. *Ibid.*, 59.

17. R. Glover, "York Boats" *The Beaver* (March 1949): 19–22.

18. John Rowand, from *The Dictionary of Canadian Biography Online* (www.biographi.ca/009004-119.01-e.php?&id_nbr=4174&interval=25&&PHPSESSID=aksq7hqecj6o9inp37db5ek1k2).

19. R.M. Ballantyne, *Hudson Bay; or, Everyday Life in the Wilds of North America*, 155.

CHAPTER 6: THE MEANDERING ECHIMAMISH

1.   The eastbound stream is not named on topographical maps of the region. It is, however, the most direct link between the Nelson River and Windy Lake. The Cree the author travelled with referred to it as the Echimamish.

2.   Halyards are used on boats to hoist and lower sails. They are usually tied around cleats in a figure-eight loop for ease of

release. On the Norway House York boat the halyards had to be tied off through an eye bolt, making release in an emergency more difficult.

3. There are remnants of four man-made dams on the Echimamish River. They were built to maintain water levels in the 1800s and 1900s by fur traders and miners. Graham Dodds, *The Hayes River, CHRS Background Study* (Ottawa: Parks Canada, 1987), 121.

4. John A. Milne, "Colony and Company, Sharing the York Mainline" *The Beaver* (Summer 1979): 4–11.

5. Divine wind is the commonly accepted translation of the Japanese word *kamikaze*. It was used to describe Japanese fighter pilots who intentionally destroyed their aircraft, and themselves, against enemy shipping in the Second World War.

Chapter 7: A Score of Beaver Dams

1. "Aurora daughter of the dawn …" Quoted from Homer, *The Iliad and Odyssey of Homer*, ed. the Rev. H.F. Cary, trans. Alexander Pope (London: George Routledge and Sons, undated edition), 337.

2. An excellent technical treatise on beavers and their dams can be found at: www.beaverdam.info/ by Steven G. Grannes, MSc.

3. The Cree call the beaver "amisk." Translation is from *Cree Syllabics Dictionary*, author unknown, 6. Photocopy of a typewritten dictionary, possibly unpublished. For additional information on Cree syllabics see www.omniglot.com/writing/cree.htm.

4. Peter C. Newman, *Company of Adventurers* (Toronto: Viking Penguin Canada, 1985), 262–264.

5. *Ibid.*, 62–65.

6. Philip Goldring, *Papers on the Labour System of the Hudson's Bay Company, 1821–1900*, Volume II, Manuscript Report

Number 412 (Ottawa: Parks Canada, 1980), 137.

7.   Réal Berard, "The Middle Track & Hayes River Route," a hand-drawn and illustrated map, published by the Manitoba Department of Natural Resources, Parks Branch.

8.   D'Arcy Jenish, *Epic Wanderer: David Thompson and the Mapping of the Canadian West* (Toronto: Anchor Canada, 2004), 35.

9.   Archibald McDonald and Malcolm McLeod, *Peace River: A Canoe Voyage from Hudson's Bay to the Pacific by the Late Sir George Simpson in 1828* (Edmonton: Hurtig, 1971), Note xl.

Chapter 8: Painted Stone and Beyond

1.   Sir John Franklin, *Journey to the Polar Sea* (Köln: Könemann, 1998), 52.

2.   *Ibid.*

3.   John A. Alwin, "Colony and Company Sharing the York Mainline" *The Beaver* (Summer 1979):4–11.

4.   In October 1821, Robert Hood was murdered by Michel Tero-haute, an Iroquois member of the Franklin expedition. Three days later, Dr. Richardson shot Terohaute to death. Robert Hood, *To the Arctic by Canoe, 1819–1821*, ed. C. Stuart Houston (Montreal and London: McGill-Queen's University Press, 1974), 147–164.

5.   Sir John Franklin, *Journey to the Polar Sea* (Köln: Könemann, 1998), 52.

6.   Robert Hood, *To the Arctic by Canoe, 1819–1821*, 34.

7.   Franklin left York Factory on September 9, 1819. He arrived at Lake Winnipeg on October 7, 1819. Sir John Franklin, *Journey to the Polar Sea*, 55.

8.   *Ibid.*

9.   Raymond M. Beaumont, *Norway House: A Brief History* (Norway House, MB: Frontier School Division No. 48, 1989), 13.

10.   Alan D. McMillan, *Native Peoples and Cultures of Canada*, 2nd ed. (Vancouver/Toronto: Douglas & McIntyre, 1995), 113.

11.   Franklin's mishap is mentioned in his *Journey to the Polar Sea*, 51, and in (Midshipman) Robert Hood's *To the Arctic by Canoe 1819–1821*, 32.

12.   Robert Hood, *To the Arctic by Canoe, 1819–1921*, 191–192.

13.   *Ibid.*, 193–194.

14.   *Ibid.*, 194–195.

15.   Sir John Franklin, *Journey to the Polar Sea*, 51.

CHAPTER 9: THE LONGEST PORTAGE

1.   Robert Hood, *To the Arctic by Canoe 1819–1821*, ed. C. Stewart Houston, (Montreal and London: McGill-Queen's University Press, 1974), Chapter II.

2.   John A. Milne, "Colony and Company Sharing the York Mainline" *The Beaver* (Summer 1979): 4–11.

3.   Dennis F. Johnson, *York Boats of the Hudson's Bay Company* (Calgary: Fifth House, 2006), 41.

4.   Graham Dodds, *The Hayes River, CHRS Background Study* (Ottawa: Parks Canada, 1987), 66.

5.   The "Song of the Volga Boatmen" is a traditional Russian barge-haulers' shanty. "*A-ay ukhnyem!*" is part of the repetitive chorus. A reasonable English translation or version would be, "Yo-o, heave ho!"

6.   Roderic Owen, *The Fate of Franklin* (London: Hutchinson, 1978), 68.

7.   Leeches are most often found in shallow, slow-moving water. They are parasites that feed on the blood of other creatures.

8.   The author wrote about the traditional Norwegian boatyard, Mellemvaerftet (Middle Wharf) in Kristiansund, in the February 1993 issue of *Classic Boat* magazine (UK), see "Boats of the

Norse," 38–41). He also mentions the yard in *Adventures with Camera and Pen* (Toronto: BookLand Press, 2009), 80.

CHAPTER 10: LOGAN LAKE AND WHITEWATER

1. In Norwegian (Norse) mythology, Thor — the god of thunder — carried a massive hammer, or axe, with which he was said to be able to level mountains. The *Prose Edda*, an old Norse collection of folk tales, tells us that, with his hammer, "Thor … would be able to strike as firmly as he wanted, whatever his aim, and the hammer would never fail, and if he threw it at something, it would never miss and never fly so far from his hand that it would not find its way back, and when he wanted, it would be so small that it could be carried inside his tunic." (en.wikipedia.org/wiki/Prose_Edda.)

2. Dr. Richardson wrote a botanical appendix to Franklin's *Journey to the Polar Sea* (Köln: Könemann, 1998), "Headed, Lichens of the Barren Grounds" (September and October, 1821). It states:

> This (*Gyrophora Muhlenbegii*) and the three preceding species (*Gyrophora proboscidea, Gyrophora hyperborean & Gyrophora pensylvanica*) were found in greater or less abundance in all rocky places throughout our journey. We used them all four as articles of food, but not having the means of extracting the bitter principle from them, they proved noxious to several of the party, producing severe bowel complaints. The Indians use *G. Muhlenbergii*, rejecting the others, and when boiled along with fish-roe or other animal matter, it is agreeable and nutritious. On the Barren

Grounds this lichen is scarce, and we were obliged to resort to the other three, which served the purpose of allaying the appetite, but were inefficient in recruiting our strength.

3. The author travelled throughout Bangladesh regularly on magazine assignments in the 1990s. During four of those visits he roamed the Sundarbans mangrove forest by boat and on foot with a Bangladeshi naturalist/photographer in search of Royal Bengal tigers.

4. Sir John Franklin, *Journey to the Polar Sea*, 50.

5. *Gouvernail* and *avant*, the traditional names for the two York boat crew members who took the steering and bow lookout positions respectively.

CHAPTER 11: NEAR DISASTER AT HELL GATES

1. Robert Hood, *To the Arctic by Canoe 1819–1821*, ed. C. Stewart Houston (Montreal and London: McGill-Queen's University Press, 1974), 32.

2. On today's trucks rope hitches are unnecessary as most loads are tied down with durable fabric strips and metal clamps, or with chains.

3. Robert Hood, *To the Arctic by Canoe 1819–1821*, 32.

4. In addition to the Nikon and a Minolta underwater camera, I had two Minolta X-700 SLR cameras with me. Due to the immersion in river water at Hell Gates, both became inoperable. I cleaned and dried them on site, as much as I could. A few weeks later at home I completely dismantled both cameras, cleaned all parts, and reassembled them. I used both cameras on subsequent assignments for years afterward. A great tribute to Minolta's engineering.

Chapter 12: Sailing on Windy Lake

1. Source: *Merriam-Webster's Collegiate Dictionary*, 10th edition (Springfield, MS: Merriam-Webster, 2001).

2. Both Lieutenant John Franklin (later Sir John) and Midshipman Robert Hood referred to the riverbanks immediately to the west of Windy Lake as the "Rabbit Ground." Sir John Franklin in *Journey to the Polar Sea* (Köln: Könemann, 1998), 50. Also Robert Hood in *To the Arctic by Canoe 1819–1821*, ed. C. Stuart Houston (Montreal and London: McGill-Queen's University Press, 1974), 31.

3. Réal Berard, "The Middle Track & Hayes River Route," a hand-drawn and illustrated map, published by the Manitoba Department of Natural Resources, Parks Branch.

4. *Lac des vents* is the French translation of "Windy Lake."

5. The quote is from Homer, *The Iliad and Odyssey of Homer*, ed. the Rev. H.F. Cary, trans. Alexander Pope (London: George Routledge and Sons, undated edition), 329.

6. In 1993, on assignment for Britain's *Classic Boat* magazine, the author sailed as a crew member on the Russian barque *Sedov*, the largest operational windjammer in the world, and later the same year on the Ukrainian barque *Tovarishch*. Both voyages are recounted in his book *Adventures with Camera and Pen* (Toronto: BookLand Press, 2009).

7. Dennis F. Johnson, *York Boats of the Hudson's Bay Company* (Calgary: Fifth House, 2006), 95. Also, R. Glover, "York Boats" *The Beaver* (March 1949): 22.

8. Sir John Franklin, *Journey to the Polar Sea* (Köln: Könemann, 1998), 49–50.

CHAPTER 13: THE WRECK AT WIPANIPANIS FALLS

1.   Sir John Franklin, *Journey to the Polar Sea* (Köln: Könemann, 1998), 49

2.   Charlie Muchikekwanape translated the name for the author.

CHAPTER 14: AN END, AND A NEW BEGINNING

1.   With reference to a boat, a double-ender is one that is shaped in such a way that both bow and stern are almost identical, as in a canoe.

2.   A keelson is a longitudinal structure running above and fastened to the keel of a ship [or boat] in order to stiffen and strengthen its framework. *Merriam Webster's Collegiate Dictionary*, 10th ed. (Springfield, MS: Merriam-Webster, 2001), 637.

3.   In August 1984, while travelling alone in the Arctic, the author's inflatable speedboat was rolled over in a storm north of Point Hope, Alaska. Anthony Dalton, *Alone Against the Arctic* (Victoria, B.C.: Heritage House, 2007).

4.   Treaty and York Boat Days are held each August in Norway House (www.nhcn.ca/yorkboatdays/index.html, accessed June 2009).

5.   Graham Dodds, *The Hayes River, CHRS Background Study* (Ottawa: Parks Canada, 1987), 69.

6.   See www.kitayan.ca/website/pages/oxford_house.html.

CHAPTER 15: THREE CANOES ON THE HAYES

1.   The author made his first overland trek from England to India in the early 1960s (hitchhiking). Subsequent journeys on many variations of the same route (in the 1970s) were in

his own four-wheel-drive Bedford truck and later in his own Land Rover.

2.   Robert Byron, *The Road to Oxiana* (London: Jonathon Cape, 1937),134.

Chapter 16: Rapid Descent

1.   Réal Berard, "The Middle Track & Hayes River Route," a hand-drawn and illustrated map, published by the Manitoba Department of Natural Resources, Parks Branch.

2.   Graham Dodds, *The Hayes River, CHRS Background Study* (Ottawa: Parks Canada, 1987), 126.

3.   R.M. Ballantyne, *Hudson Bay; or, Everyday Life in the Wilds of North America.* (London: Thomas Nelson & Sons, 1901), 231.

4.   *Ibid.*, 232.

5.   *Ibid.*, 233.

6.   The Rock is actually a series of large flat rocks in the middle of the river. The main flow of water falls over a rocky ledge to the right of the islands.

7.   Réal Berard, "The Middle Track & Hayes River Route."

8.   Hap Wilson and Stephanie Ackroyd, *Wilderness Rivers of Manitoba* (Merrickville, ON: Recreational Canoeing Association, 1998), 90–104.

9.   R.M. Ballantyne. *Hudson Bay; or, Everyday Life in the Wilds of North America*, 228.

Chapter 17: Final Days on the Mighty River

1.   Franklin referred to Borrowick's Fall in *Journey to the Polar Sea* (Köln: Könemann, 1998). Réal Berard refers to the locations as Borthwick or Borrowick Rapids in "The Middle Track

& Hayes River Route" (Manitoba Department of Natural Resources, Parks Branch). Modern topographical maps use Berwick Falls.

2. Réal Berard, "The Middle Track & Hayes River Route."
3. The television series was *Great Canadian Rivers*. The Hayes River segment was one episode.
4. R.M. Ballantyne, *Hudson Bay; or, Everyday Life in the Wilds of North America* (London: Thomas Nelson & Sons, 1901), 98–105.
5. *Ibid.*, 166.
6. *Ibid.*, 213.
7. Réal Berard, "The Middle Track & Hayes River Route."
8. *Ibid.*
9. The quote is from Homer, *The Iliad and Odyssey of Homer*, ed. the Rev. H.F. Cary, trans. Alexander Pope (London: George Routledge and Sons, undated edition), 407.

CHAPTER 18: YORK FACTORY

1. Parks Canada's website has a wealth of information on York Factory. www.pc.gc.ca.
2. Peter. C. Newman, *Company of Adventurers* (Toronto: Viking Penguin Canada, 1985), 48–49.
3. *Ibid.*, 143–164.
4. *Ibid.*, 195.
5. Harold A. Innis, *The Fur Trade in Canada*, revised edition (Toronto: University of Toronto Press, 1956), 290–293.
6. Selkirk settlers: J.M. Bumsted, *Lord Selkirk, A Life* (Winnipeg: University of Manitoba Press, 2008), 204–206.
7. R.M. Ballantyne, *Hudson Bay; or, Everyday Life in the Wilds of North America* (London: Thomas Nelson & Sons, 1901), 41.
8. *Ibid.*, 48.

9. *Ibid.*, 167.

10. Robert Hood, *To the Arctic by Canoe 1819–1821*, ed. C. Stuart Houston (Montreal and London: McGill-Queen's University Press, 1974), 21.

11. Information on many HBC ships can be in the HBC Archives in Winnipeg, (www.gov.mb.ca).

12. Composite, in the sense of *Pelican*'s construction, refers to her hull being built from two quite different materials. In this case, almost certainly a wooden hull over iron frames.

13. Harold A. Innis, *The Fur Trade in Canada*, 121–122.

14. Information on A.B. McIvor is from "The Middle Track & Hayes River Route," a hand-drawn map by Réal Berard and published by the Manitoba Department of Natural Resources, Parks Branch.

15. "If the treasure to which we had the key …" comes from the third verse of the Louis Dudek translation of Quebec singer/songwriter/poet Gilles Vigneault's romantic poem "*Si les bateaux*" ("If all the ships …").

BIBLIOGRAPHY

Books

Ballantyne, R.M. *Hudson Bay; or, Everyday Life in the Wilds of North America*. London: Thomas Nelson & Sons, 1901.

Berton, Pierre. *Klondike: The Last Great Gold Rush 1896–1899*. Toronto: McClelland & Stewart, 1972.

Bumsted, J.M. *Lord Selkirk: A Life*. Winnipeg: University of Manitoba Press, 2008.

Byron, Robert. *The Road to Oxiana*. London: Jonathan Cape, 1937.

Campey, Lucille H. *The Silver Chief, Lord Selkirk and the Scottish Pioneers of Belfast, Baldoon and Red River*. Toronto: Natural Heritage Books, 2003.

Conrad, Joseph. *The Mirror of the Sea*. New edition. Plainview, NY: The Marlborough Press, 1988.

Dalton, Anthony. *Adventures with Camera and Pen.* Toronto: Book-Land Press, 2009.

Finkelstein, Max, and James Stone. *Paddling the Boreal Forest, Rediscovering A.P. Low.* Toronto: Natural Heritage Books, 2004.

Franklin, Sir John. *Narrative of a Journey to the Shores of the Polar Sea.* London: Murray, 1823. A later edition, *Journey to the Shores of the Polar Sea,* was published (in English) by Könemann Verlagsgesellschaft mbH, Köln, Germany, 1998.

Hodgins, Bruce W., and Margaret Hobbs, eds. *Nastawgan: The Canadian North by Canoe & Snowshoe.* Toronto: Dundurn Press, 1987.

Homer. *The Iliad and Odyssey of Homer.* Translated by Alexander Pope and edited by the Rev. H.F. Cary. London and New York: George Routledge and Sons. Undated hardcover edition in the Excelsior Series.

Hood, Robert. *To the Arctic by Canoe 1819–1821.* Edited by C. Stuart Houston. Montreal and London: McGill-Queen's University Press, 1974.

Innis, Harold A. *The Fur Trade in Canada.* Revised edition. Toronto: University of Toronto Press, 1956.

Jenish, D'Arcy. *Epic Wanderer, David Thompson and the Mapping of the Canadian West.* Toronto: Anchor Canada, 2004.

Johnson, Dennis F. *York Boats of the Hudson's Bay Company, Canada's Inland Armada.* Calgary: Fifth House, 2006.

Jones, Tristan. *To Venture Further.* New York: Hearst Marine Books, 1991.

McGoogan, Ken. *Fatal Passage: The Untold Story of John Rae, the Arctic Adventurer Who Discovered the Fate of Franklin.* Toronto: HarperFlamingo Canada, 2001.

_____. *Ancient Mariner: The Amazing Adventures of Samuel Hearne, the Sailor Who Walked to the Arctic Ocean.* Toronto: HarperFlamingo Canada, 2003.

McMillan, Alan D. *Native Peoples and Cultures of Canada,* 2nd edition. Vancouver/Toronto: Douglas & McIntyre, 1995.

Mowat, Farley. *Tundra.* Toronto: McClelland & Stewart, 1973.

Newman, Peter C. *Company of Adventurers.* Toronto: Viking Penguin Canada, 1985

_____. *Caesars of the Wilderness.* Viking Penguin Canada, Toronto, 1987.

_____. *Empire of the Bay.* Toronto: Madison Press, 1989.

_____. *Merchant Princes.* Toronto: Toronto: Viking Penguin Canada, 1991.

Owen, Roderick. *The Fate of Franklin.* London: Hutchinson, 1978.

Raffan, James. *Emperor of the North: Sir George Simpson and the Remarkable Story of the Hudson's Bay Company.* Toronto: HarperCollins, 2007.

Robertson, Heather. *Measuring Mother Earth: How Joe the Kid Became Tyrrell of the North*. Toronto: McClelland & Stewart, 2007.

Scot, Barbara J. *The Stations of Still Creek*. San Francisco: Sierra Club, 1999.

Schooling, Sir William. *The Hudson's Bay Company, 1670–1920*. London: Hudson's Bay Company, 1920.

Spencer, Charles. *Prince Rupert: The Last Cavalier*. London: Weidenfeld and Nicolson, 2007.

Thompson, David. *Travels in Western North America, 1784–1812*. Edited. by Victor G. Hopwood. Toronto: Macmillan of Canada, 1971.

Wilson, Hap. *Trails and Tribulations*. Toronto: Natural Heritage Books/ Dundurn Press, 2009.

_____, and Stephanie Ackroyd. *Wilderness Rivers of Manitoba*. Merrickville, ON: Canadian Recreational Canoeing Association, 1998.

Articles and Papers

Alwin, John A. "Colony and Company, Sharing the York Mainline." *The Beaver* (Summer 1979): 4–11.

Beaumont, Raymond M. *Norway House: A Brief History*. Norway House, MB: Frontier School Division, No. 48., 1989.

Boggiss, Dorothy L. "York Boat Coming." *The Beaver* (June 1954): 50–51.

Dalton, Anthony. "Rapid Descent." *(*www.wildernesspirit.com).

Dodds, Graham. *The Hayes River, Canadian Heritage Rivers System Background Study.* Ottawa: Parks Canada, 1987.

Glover, R. "York Boats." *The Beaver* (March 1949): page 1923.

Goldring, Philip. *Papers on the Labour System of the Hudson's Bay Company, 1821–1900.* Volume II, Manuscript Report Number 412. Ottawa: Parks Canada, 1980.

King, William Cornwallis. "North with the Red River Brigade." *The Beaver* (August/September 1995): 34–36.

Manitoba Department of Natural Resources. "Prehistory of the Bay Area." Undated.

Parks Canada website. "York Factory National Historic Sites of Canada." (www.pc.gc.ca.)

Ready, W.B. "Norway House." *The Beaver* (March 1949).

Ross, Bernard Rogan. "Fur Trade Gossip Sheet." *The Beaver* (Spring 1955): 52–3

Spencer, Anne Ellen (Mrs. R.F. Inkster). "To School in England." *The Beaver* (Summer 1979): 43–49.

"The Packet." (Letters) *The Beaver* (Spring 1955): 54–55.

Unknown author. *Cree Syllabics Dictionary.* Author unknown. Photocopy of a typewritten dictionary, possibly unpublished.

Williams, Glyndwr. "The Hudson's Bay Company and the Fur Trade: 1670–1870." *The Beaver*, Special Issue (Autumn 1983).

INDEX

ABOUT THE AUTHOR
Anthony Dalton

ANTHONY DALTON IS AN ADVENTURER and an author. In the 1970s he led regular expeditions driving four-wheel-drive vehicles into and across the Sahara, through the deserts of the Middle East, and into the mountainous terrain of Afghanistan. In 1980 he was the organizer and leader of a CBC filming expedition from Bamako via Mopti and Timbuktu to the Saharan salt mines of Taoudenit in northern Mali. In 1984 he survived capsizing in a violent storm while travelling hundreds of nautical miles along the Arctic coast of northwestern Alaska alone in an inflatable speedboat. The early 1990s saw Dalton switch his attention to the rivers of the Sundarbans jungle of Bangladesh to track Royal Bengal tigers in their natural habitat, and in 1994 he joined twelve members of the Cree First Nation on a traditional York boat voyage on Manitoba's historic Hayes River between Norway House and Oxford House. While canoeing the second half of the Hayes River from Oxford House to York Factory on Hudson Bay in 2000, he participated in a television documentary on great Canadian rivers for the Discovery Channel.

He has written six non-fiction books and collaborated on two others in addition to publishing articles in magazines and newspapers in twenty countries and nine languages. Anthony Dalton is a fellow of the Royal Geographical Society, fellow of the Explorers Club, national president of the Canadian Authors Association, member of The Writers' Union of Canada, and a member of the Welsh Academi.

OF RELATED INTEREST

Trails and Tribulations
Confessions of a Wilderness Pathfinder
by Hap Wilson
978-1-55488-397-4
$26.99

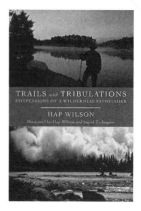

In an age when "survival" shows permeate the media, noted northern traveller Hap Wilson shares accounts of his lifelong involvement with wilderness living within the Canadian Shield. Wilson knows better than most how to live in the woods and has also learned from first-hand experience that nature can neither be beaten nor tamed. *Trails and Tribulations* takes the reader on a journey with the author through natural settings ranging from austere to mysterious and breathtaking, and the inevitable dangers including animal attacks, bushfires, and hypothermia.

The Lure of Faraway Places
Reflections on Wilderness and Solitude
by Herb Pohl
978-1-897045-24-4
$27.95

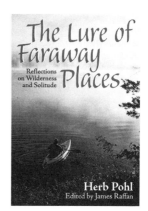

The Lure of Faraway Places is the publication canoeist Herb Pohl (1930–2006) did not live to see published. But Pohl, remembered as "Canada's most remarkable solo traveller," left behind words and images that provide a unique portrait of Canada by one who was happiest when travelling our northern waterways alone.

...ing a Continent
...n the Trail of Alexander Mackenzie
by Max Finkelstein
978-1-896219-00-4
$25.95

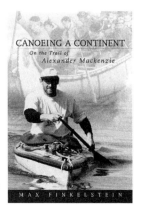

A highly personal account of the travels of Max
Finkelstein as he retraces, some two hundred
years later, the route of Alexander Mackenzie,
the first European to cross North America
(1793). Using Mackenzie's journals and his own journal writings,
the author followed the route of Alexander Mackenzie across North
America from Ottawa through to Cumberland House, Saskatchewan,
and paddled the Blackwater, Fraser, and Peace Rivers, completing the
trip in 1999. This route is the most significant water trail in North
America, and perhaps the world.

Available at your favourite bookseller.

DUNDURN PRESS
www.dundurn.com

Tell us your story! What did you think of this book?
Join the conversation at www.definingcanada.ca/tell-your-story
by telling us what you think.